THE IDENTITY CRISIS

THE *identity* CRISIS

The Search for Identity in a World of Darkness

MONICA WICKER-RAMSAY

© 2017 by Monica Wicker-Ramsey. All rights reserved.

Published by Redemption Press, PO Box 427, Enumclaw, WA 98022 Toll Free (844) 2REDEEM (273-3336)

Redemption Press is honored to present this title in partnership with the author. The views expressed or implied in this work are those of the author. Redemption Press provides our imprint seal representing design excellence, creative content, and high quality production.

No part of this publication may be reproduced, stored in a retrieval system, or transmitted in any way by any means—electronic, mechanical, photocopy, recording, or otherwise—without the prior permission of the copyright holder, except as provided by USA copyright law.

Unless otherwise noted, all Scripture is taken from the King James Version.

Verses marked NKJV are taken from the New King James Version®. Copyright © 1982 by Thomas Nelson, Inc. Used by permission. All rights reserved.

Verses marked NIV are taken from the Holy Bible, New International Version®, NIV®. Copyright © 1973, 1978, 1984, 2011 by Biblical, Inc. ®Used by permission. All rights reserved worldwide.

Verses marked AMP are taken from The Amplified Bible, Copyright © 1954, 1958, 1962, 1964, 1965, 1987 by The Lockman Foundation. All rights reserved. Used by permission. (www.Lockman.org)

Verses marked NLT are taken from the Holy Bible, New Living Translation, copyright ©1996, 2004, 2007, 2013 by Tyndale House Foundation. Used by permission of Tyndale House Publishers, Inc., Carol Stream, Illinois 60188. All rights reserved.

Verses marked NASB are taken from the New American Standard Bible®, © 1960, 1962, 1963, 1968, 1971, 1972, 1973, 1975, 1977, 1995 by The Lockman Foundation. Used by permission. (www.Lockman.org)

All emphasis in Scripture has been added by the author, and all italics and bold in Scriptures have been added by the author.

Subscripts are provided to make it easy to correlate cited references with the reference page.

ISBN 13: 978-1-68314-412-0

Library of Congress Catalog Card Number: 2017957095

DEDICATION

I would first like to dedicate this book to my Savior, Jesus Christ. I also dedicate this book to my parents and my awesome brothers. You have always been supportive of my dreams and believed in me when I did not believe in myself. To my husband and my dear son, Joshua, I also dedicate this book to you. Thank you for your love and support.

To my closest friends: Thank you for your love, support, and how you encouraged me to pursue God and my dreams. Last, but not least, I dedicate this book to my late brother-in-law, Deryck. Deryck was one of the few people that I felt safe enough to be vulnerable with to share my truest dreams. My sincerest thanks to Deryck for making me believe I can do all the things that I have dreamed in my heart to do. I am privy to the fact that Deryck wanted to write a book before he left this world, so I dedicate this book to honor him and his dream.

CONTENTS

Introduction	1
Section One: The One Identity Crisis That Breeds All Others	5
Chapter 1 Lost Identity	7
Chapter 2 The Genesis Of Your Identity Crisis	17
Chapter 3 Understanding Strongholds	29
Chapter 4 The Lazarus Effect	41
Section Two: Three Roadblocks To Discovering Your Identity	49
Chapter 5 Satan: Your Adversary	51
Chapter 6 The World: The Celestial Collision	59
Chapter 7 The Flesh: The Battle Within	67
Section Three: The Seat Of All Affection: Your Soul	73
Chapter 8 Self-Imprisonment	75
Chapter 9 The Emotions	83
Chapter 10 The Will	89
Section Four: "The Art Of War"	97
Chapter 11 Understanding The Battle	99
Chapter 12 You Have The Advantage	107
Chapter 13 Change Your Thinking	117
Chapter 14 Change Your Speaking	129
Chapter 15 Change Your Heart	143
Section Five: Discovering Your True Identity	153
Chapter 16 Jesus Christ, Your Example	155
Chapter 17 Jesus Christ Realizing His Identity	167
Chapter 18 What This Means for You: Your Spiritual Inheritance	175
Chapter 19 Conclusion: The New You	191
Dream And Visions Interpretation Guide	199
References	217

INTRODUCTION

Life is mysterious, unpredictable, and filled with ambiguity. It is in the moments of the uncertainties of life that we find ourselves searching for clarity and resolutions to life's dilemmas. At times, life casts its darkness on us and we become lost in the vastness of its expanse. We go from living to just existing. The darkness begins to define who we are as it sifts our hope, our passion, and our joyful optimism for life, leaving us hollow. These spans of darkness, which I call night seasons, can be engulfing, rendering us powerless and debilitated.

In most instances, night seasons of life can seem to linger too long, causing us to have thoughts of inferiority and feelings of hopelessness, inadequacy, and great perplexity. Have you ever felt at times like you were losing your grip on life? I have . . . I know what it's like to feel powerless. There were times I beheld myself in the mirror and felt disdain as my life spiraled out of control. I have often gazed in the mirror and wondered: Who am I? Am I capable of lasting change? Will I ever be truly happy? Is there more to life? Questions always surface in darkness, which poses a quandary that is difficult to solve in the absence of self-actualization or self-realization. Being void of an accurate awareness of one's identity breeds an identity crisis. If left undiscovered, the crisis can morph into your identity. But you are not your crisis. You are so much more! In you lies greatness; thus, insight regarding your identity is essential to you being able to realize and release the greatness that is already inside you.

Do you know that an identity crisis can occur at any stage and at any age in life, and that the crisis can last years—even decades? An identity crisis is an inevitable phase of life. You have to take responsibility for this phase regardless. You have to decide if you will continue in life having an identity crisis, or if you will come out of life an overcomer of the identity crisis, having ascertained your true identity. I am confident that many of you can identify with the struggle to gain a sense of self and the pain that is associated with the struggle. I hope I have found you at a point in life where you are exhausted with the struggle, tired of the ordinary, and weary of missing out on the abundant life that you know God has for you. I want to share with you some powerful keys that were revealed to me through my personal struggles and anguish. I want to encourage you: No matter how unbearably tangled your problems may seem, or how much pain you're in, the message I will share in this book will unlock layers of your soul and bring incredible freedom and healing to your innermost parts.

I have to be honest: Much of this book was birthed from a deeply personal and arduous journey. I went through a major identity crisis in my own life—one that I wasn't sure I would come out of. It was not until the sheer reality of my daily existing in utter unhappiness, feeling beaten down and totally exhausted from the dread and fear of what people thought of me, that a chord struck deep inside. Finally, at my breaking point, I said, "Enough is enough!" And I believe my breakthrough was marked at that moment—the minute I refused to go another day letting myself be deprived of life. I began to run with all I had after the life God has for me, which was foreordained even before I was born! I became determined that I would live this life to the fullest and I want to wholeheartedly and emphatically encourage you that you can, too!

Many of the truths I will share with you in this book are compilations of personal experiences, things I have seen in the lives of others, and revelations given to me from heaven by the very inspiration of God. These illuminations were given to me through the Word of God, and through dreams and visions from God during different seasons in my life throughout the last five years. The Word of God tells us that in the last days, "I will pour out My Spirit upon all flesh; and your sons and daughters shall prophesy, your old men shall dream dreams, your young men shall see visions."(Joel 2:28) So, before you recoil from the proclamation that the truths I will share with you in this book are from God, let me share with you another scripture. As written in the book of Job, "For God may speak in one way, or in another, yet man does not perceive it. In a dream, in vision of the night, when deep sleep falls upon men, while slumbering on their beds, then he opens the ears of men, and seals their instruction."(Job 33:14-16 NKJV) God will often use the stillness of the night when all is free from life's distractions to enter our world and reveal his thoughts and his plans. "Why?" you may ask. It is simply because he loves you so dearly. He wants you to know who you are in him in order to come to that identity realization and actualization, for your purpose and destiny in life are tied to your identity. Discovering your true identity will equip you for the plans God has for your life.

Upon the completion of this book, I felt strongly urged in my spirit to make a Dreams and Visions Interpretation Guide (which you will find at the back of this book). As we journey together in unpacking the truth about what God has to say concerning identity, you will also receive keys in this book to help you learn the spiritual language of dreams and visions. Knowing how to understand dreams and visions will help deepen your dialogue with God as you journey together with Him to realize and actualize your identity. I pray that the content contained in this book will stretch your spiritual tent to help you house more of what God wants to give you. (Isaiah 54:2) I pray also that after you finish this book, you will discover your true identity and live in joyful optimism with God and His plans for your life. May you go from surviving the darkness to thriving in the light of your identity. May you know God and who you are in Him!

SECTION ONE

The One Identity Crisis that Breeds All Others

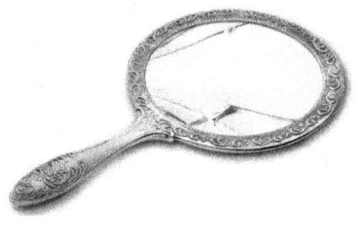

CHAPTER ONE

Lost Identity

1
Lost Identity

One night, some Christians decided to gather for a time of prayer and intercession; they gathered in anticipation of having a great night of prayer and fellowship. Then suddenly, a woman staggered into the room. She made her way through the corridor, down the aisle to the front of the room, and flopped across the front row with her hands covering her face and her foot dangling off the chair. I turned around and saw the woman lying there. I looked to see if anyone knew the woman. No one knew her. She didn't come to harm anyone, she just desperately wanted prayer. This woman was an alcoholic who was living in poverty.

I noticed the woman was a petite lady wearing all black. I could tell she was in her seventies. I noticed her wrinkled skin; she had lived a hard life. Somehow without words or judgment, we made our way over to this woman and began to pray. One of the women in our group reached out her hand to touch the lady, and when she did, she uttered these earth-shattering words, "God said you were supposed to be a healer to many people." The woman remained there in a heap with her hands still covering her face. And though the message that she was "supposed to be a healer" to hundreds of thousands of people implied she had missed her life's calling, we continued to pray for her; we still felt there was hope for her, a hope that only God could give.

The Cost of Not Knowing Your Identity

This dream left me speechless in the morning. I knew this dream was from God so I asked Him what it meant. In short, in this dream the woman was older in years and much of her life had been ravaged by pain and disappointments from which she tried to self-medicate through alcohol consumption. This woman was meant to be more in life. God had a purpose and plan for her. This woman, potentially, could have held the cure for cancer, AIDS, or even Alzheimer's on the inside of her--the world will never know. She failed to become a great healer because it was easier to believe in a lie that she was a woman of no value, no worth, a woman who could not succeed at anything in life. Years of pain and disappointment validated this erroneous narrative for her—or at least she allowed it to.

I came to realize this dream was a representation of all the people who have failed or will fail to reach their destiny in life because they did not know their true identity. What are you doing with your time? The Lord once asked me this sobering question and now I ask you the same. What are you doing with your time? How you spend your time in life matters. Making good use of your time is wise, but using your time poorly will cost you. It cost this woman a fulfilling life.

Oddly enough, we felt hopeful for this woman in the dream because with God, there is always hope. As long as there is breath in your body, you still have a chance to do something great in life. "With God all things are possible." (Matthew 19:26) I love what Terri Savelle Foy, Christian motivational speaker, always says, "Don't look at the years you lost, look at the years you've got left." Your past doesn't have to determine your future. You are not your past failures nor are you your bad habits; you are so much more than you know.

This woman's purpose in life was that of a healer, but she never realized it because she did not know her true self. You see, knowing your identity is the foundation from which your life is to be built upon. Your identity is tied to your purpose and your purpose is tied to your destiny. Your identity is the launching pad from which you were designed to blast off into your purpose; your purpose is the orbit that leads to your destiny. Life is filled with choices and the consequences of those choices. The ultimate decision you will face is whether you will merely exist in this life, or live the life God has for you. You have only one life; choose to live it!

Where Am I?

On a lighter note, after being a stay-at-home mom for about four years, I decided to find some part-time work so I could get out of the house a bit. So, I started work at a senior home in the assisted living industry. After about two months of working, I was starting to get familiar with the residents who lived at the facility, in particular those who lived on the first floor, as I was assigned to them most often.

One day, I arrived at work to find nearly all of the residents rapt with enjoyment as they were being entertained by a group of volunteer teenage musicians. All the residents were basking in the music, and I, in efficient fashion, thought, *This is great! I can get ahead and get things prepared before dinner time.* It was then that I saw this man I hadn't seen before wandering around looking puzzled. The man finally approached me and asked if I knew this guy, "Walter" (Name changed for sake of confidentiality). The man went on to tell me he had been looking for Walter, a friend he came to visit. Well, I didn't know Walter. However, I assured this man that I would help him look for Walter's room. The man was very appreciative.

I looked and looked for Walter's room, but could not find it. I even asked a coworker if she knew Walter and where his room was—but to no avail; we could not find Walter! As we were searching, the gentleman seemed a bit frustrated and confused that no one could find Walter. I'm sure he thought, *These idiots work here and can't find their resident, Walter!* He was adamant about the fact that Walter had moved to the facility. The man finally accepted the fact that we couldn't find his friend, and I guess he decided to go find someone who could. After dinner, a visiting guest inquired about a new resident. The guest wanted to know how the resident was adjusting to the facility, what meds he was taking, And whether he experienced any changes in his physical and mental health since his arrival at the facility.

The visitor said that the resident had seemed a little disoriented and that was not his norm. Well, you wouldn't believe who the visitor was inquiring about . . . it was Walter. Come to find out, this man was a new resident and his name was Walter. Walter was looking for Walter! You can imagine my befuddlement when I realized that Walter was in fact Walter; it was his nickname, but Walter nonetheless. He had been trying to find himself for over an hour. When I couldn't help Walter find himself, he became so frustrated—and I mean downright dejected. Poor thing, he was confused and I confused him even more. Turned out, his confusion was a side effect of the meds he was prescribed. But I have to be honest, I had a few laughs about the situation.

On my day off I began to think about old Walter looking intently for himself for hours, and when no one would or could tell him what he wanted to hear about Walter, he became terribly frustrated and disappointed. I began to think, *Now how ironic is that?* The truth is, there are many people in the same boat as Walter. How often do many of us wander throughout life in search of ourselves? When met with obstacles and unforeseen circumstances that should offer clarity about our identity, we find that they only leave us more frustrated than we were. We become displaced, disappointed, defeated, and yes, downright dejected.

When uncertain, we so often look to others to provide clarity about who we are, but any efforts to gain an understanding of your true self outside of God will only leave you wanting, and more confused about who you are. I have found that many people are not aware of what it is they are devoid of—hence, never getting to the root of their disappointments nor their frustration with life. Metaphorically speaking, many people walk up to others all through life looking for themselves, asking others, *Can you help me find myself?* Many become dependent on others to aid them in their quest for answers to identity concerns, looking for affirmation and even validation as to who they really are. Many are lost because they have not found themselves. When we are blind to the truth that our identity comes from God and is in God, we spiral into an identity crisis.

What Is Identity?

Before we can establish what an identity crisis is, we must first understand the meaning of identity, and how identity is formed. I personally define identity in this manner: *the distinctiveness, uniqueness, and continuity of one's individuality in attributes, personality, character, and purpose in life.* There are various forms of identity. There is gender identity, racial identity, national identity, cultural identity, and individual identity to name a few. One's gender, race, and nation of birth are aspects of an identity that help to define the distinctiveness, personality, and attributes of a person.

Culture identity is made up of two or more persons that share the same values and beliefs. Within cultures we see sub-cultures that hold shared values and beliefs. A self-culture is also an identity. It is one person that holds a certain belief that goes against culture; their beliefs and values stands alone. A self-culture is an identity of one that is a by-product of a greater culture but is individualistic and unique. The development of identity is a blend of many aspects that are shaped by one's surroundings, education, influences, awareness, geographical location, etc. Despite the many types of identity we will be focusing on personal identity throughout this book. Your personal identity is the key to your happiness and wholeness in life. Now let's get a better understanding for how an identity is formed.

The on-set of identity formation takes shape at the point of conception, something so miraculous and unique takes shape inside a woman who has conceived. From the time her newborn baby enters the world, he or she begins a lifelong journey of exploration of the world around them, and little by little, they become familiar with their surroundings and begin to make sense of their environment. As infants grow and mature, so does their worldview. The way they view their world is defined by moments in life. Every experience they encounter becomes a lens through which they view, know, and understand the world around them. A philosophy of life takes shape during childhood and follows the child throughout life. So, it becomes apparent that every external encounter molds a child from infancy to adulthood; forming the identity.

The Development of Personality and Character

Let's look at personality and character development. When a child enters the world, he or she is a genius at being themselves. With children, you witness openness, purity of thought, curiosity, and uniqueness. Personality takes shape right before your eyes. Children aren't afraid to just "be." This is all they know. Having worked with people on the opposite end of the spectrum in the senior industry, I have seen some of the same attributes among the elderly. I have had conversations with family members and staff about how certain residents are so sweet and funny, some timid, and others downright ornery. I have heard family members say things like, "Mom used to be mean," or, "Mom was very quiet and strict all her life." They see Mom in the assisted living being sweet, considerate of others, and funny, and they can't fully understand this drastic change in personality. I find that family members are happy to see this side of their parents, but wonder why they never encountered this side previously throughout their younger lives.

I thought about this and the old adage came to mind, "Once a man, twice a child." Now, we can be technical about the meaning of this saying, but allow me to help you to see it in another light. Children have no need for pretense; what you see is what you get. As we age and come to the last years of life, we realize the diminutive nature of life. The elderly begin to experience a visceral connection to themselves, others, and life. They find that there is no longer any need to be compromising, or disingenuous. For example, what can appear in some seniors as mean-spiritedness, or being sharp and insensitive in speech is in actuality, authenticity. The need for pretense goes out the window and what you see is what you get.

On the contrary, somewhere between the gap of childhood entering adulthood, along life's continuum, we lose our authentic self. The individuality and uniqueness of our personality is blemished as we become adults. We become conscious of the world around us, its prerequisites, expectations, and limitations. It is between the years of childhood and the time we become advanced in years that many either rise to a forged pedestal and put on airs (superiority), or succumb to the negativity of life (inferiority). Somewhere between these opposing positions of superiority and inferiority lies a balance where we see ourselves for who we are, we understand whose we are, and we know what we are meant for. The *between* is the core, the central focus where we strike the chords of balance and equilibrium within the identity; not thinking of ourselves more highly than we ought (Roman 12:3), but thinking with thoughts that are sober and accurate depictions of our true identity.

What Is An Identity Crisis?

An identity crisis *is a personal psychological and social crisis resulting in confusion about one's self value, role in society, and purpose in life.* In an attempt to excavate the identity, we erroneously pinpoint the "self" based on identifiers. "Identifiers" are attributes used to characterize us, but they do not, nor can they indicate who we really are. For example, we think our identity is determined by our thoughts, feelings, behaviors, profession, ethnicity, sexual orientation, successes, failures, socioeconomic standing, and so on, which are identifiers. But who is the *you* that thinks your thoughts? Who is the *you* that feels your emotions? Who is the *you* that is deeper than the color of your skin? Who are you? More often than not, we have oppositions within identifiers. We have conflict in our thoughts and emotions that impact how we think and feel about ourselves. For example, some people have divergences in working a profession they are not happy with, consequently experiencing opposition within identifiers. Opposition within identifiers leads to the deformation of our true identity. Distorted perceptions of self brings into being an unresolved crisis of identity. An unresolved identity crisis will spread into every aspect of your life. It will impede your relational, mental, emotional, physical, and spiritual well-being.

When stuck with distorted views of who you are, you are left ignorant about your true self. Deprivation of identity makes it difficult to continue on life's journey effectively. Lacking a true sense of identity will cause you to wander aimlessly, never fully attaining the life God has in store for you. Our adversary is persistent and patient. Satan starts early, from the onset. As children enter the world, he begins to attack the identity. He then works within our identifiers—within our surroundings, using people closest to us, and our environment—society—to thwart the development of our identity. The gap between the purity of childhood and the experiences of the aged is breached, and this causes disruption and instability in personality and purpose in life. In this phase, the distinctiveness, uniqueness, and individuality of personality and purpose for many is nowhere to be found. *Your identity was never meant to be lost but rather to be understood, attained, and evolving.* Knowing your identity is the most priceless possession you will ever have in life. Your identity is tied to your purpose. *Your identity will carve out a niche for you in this world; it will give you the confidence you need to be uniquely you, while propelling you toward the purposes and plans of God for your life*. Together, we will recover and reclaim the purity and uniqueness of your identity, giving you the freedom to be who you are in the eyes of God in this world.

Journey with Me

I will go so far as to say I guarantee the truths and practical dispositions contained within this book will work for you, if you earnestly and diligently apply them. The transformation inside that you are seeking will not happen overnight; what you get depends upon how much you put into it. The revelatory keys in this book will arm you with powerful tools to live by and weapons to fight with. Be willing to surrender daily any discouragement or frustration that arises and receive God's grace and unconditional love for you on your journey to discovering your identity. Enter into each day with an attitude of expectant anticipation that as you open your heart to freedom and growth, God will meet you there in a powerful way. If you are ready, then make that choice and stick with it . . . I know you can!! Now, let's go!

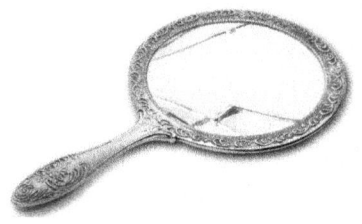

CHAPTER TWO

The Genesis of Your Identity Crisis

2
The Genesis of Your Identity Crisis

In the pastoral play, *As You Like It*, the renowned William Shakespeare wrote these words, "All the world's a stage, and all the men and women merely players" (lines 139-140).[1] In essence, Shakespeare was alluding to the fact that we are all just actors on a stage. One can see how his poetic analogy can be perceived as insightful. In the grand theater of life, we are all issued scripts to live by. These scripts are screen written by culture, society, and the people in our lives. They tell us how we should look, how we should feel, how we should think, and what we should do in order to be successful and contribute to society.

In life, we take on different roles and play various parts until we arrive at a point in life where the script no longer fits the scene. The landscape of life changes and we are left bewildered. We begin to wonder, *What do I do now? Who am I? What am I passionate about? What is my purpose in life?* We become disoriented concerning ourselves, God, and our purpose in life. Here lies the identity crisis. Our identity suffers at the hands of many because we fail to take the hand of the only One who can reveal what is concealed about our identity—our God, the Creator. Who knows more about creation then its creator? Now think on that for just a moment.

Identity Crisis

The term *identity crisis* was coined by Erik Erikson. Erikson is well-known for his theoretical framework on the stages of psychosocial development throughout life, from infancy to old age. This stage theory offers a premise that the social relationships we have with others have a direct impact on our psychological (mental and emotional) development. The link between our social interactions and our mental and emotional state shapes of our identity. In essence social dynamics fashions who we are. Erikson, Abraham Maslow, Carl Rogers, and others made great contributions to the field of human development as it relates to the study of identity development. We will touch on some of these theories in subsequent chapters; however, it is important to note that Erikson's research led him to put "a great deal of emphasis on the adolescent period, feeling it was a crucial stage for developing a person's identity."[2] Now, I know this is a huge assertion to be made, but this was Erikson's assertion.

Erikson focused his school of thought on the identity crisis being a stage that is experienced during adolescence years, believing that the success of identity formation in adolescence is determined by how successful the adolescent progress is from its inception in previous stages of psychosocial development, beginning from birth through childhood. When an adolescent person acquires a sense of identity, the identity crisis is resolved, and it will allow the adolescent to be successful in adulthood. On the other hand, if the identity crisis is not resolved because the adolescent did not advance from one stage of development to the next successfully, adulthood will be filled with turmoil and disarray.

Although I do not hold firmly to Erikson's assertion 100%, I do agree with the premise that the development of identity is a vital and crucial stage in life. The identity of an individual is foundational to a sense of self that either begets a life of happiness, meaning, and fulfillment—or propagates the polar opposite. According to Erikson, a crisis can occur at every stage in life; albeit, Erikson emphasized that the crisis of the identity occurs during the adolescence stage of life. On the contrary, I do believe the crisis of identity is more prevalent in the lives of adults than what has been statistically verified in the field of psychology. In fact, an identity crisis can be brought on at different stages of human development, and it can be brought on by a plethora of events. Everyone who has suffered or will suffer an identity crisis has their own adverse circumstances that are unique to them, and the onset of the crisis may be caused by various events and can come at any time

The Onset of Identity Crisis

Different stages in life and a range of events can trigger (start) an identity crisis. I have talked with a few people who have experienced some of the crises I will discuss in detail in this section. Many have shared that after experiencing and coming out of these crises they found themselves dealing with emotional baggage they never had prior to the crisis. Based on real-life experiences such as these and my own, I have determined that the onset of an identity crisis is more widespread in adulthood than noted. Below are some examples of stages—events in life that trigger an identity crisis: the adolescence stage, sexual molestation or rape, marriage, divorce, the empty nest syndrome, transitional crises, severing of friendships, midlife crisis, and retirement. These are some, certainly not all, of the main events that cause crises.

Adolescent Years

First let's look at the adolescent stage of life. During the adolescent years, teens begin the process of discovering a sense of self by exploring the world around them. They examine their beliefs, values, and things they like to do in life through the lens of interaction with their peers. Friendships during teen years are important. Having people to relate to and connect with helps teens feel accepted in the world. Teens also enter an awkward phase when they start experiencing changes in their body. They go through a process of trying to understand their bodies, their role in society based on social association, the ability to relate to others, and social acceptance. Failure to identify their identity and role results in a crisis of the identity and confusion about their role in society.

Sexual Molestation/Rape

Sexual molestation is a sexual crime that is carried out on children under the age of 18. Sexual molestation and rape create a serious identity crisis in the lives of its victims who often wrestle with feelings of guilt and shame. They often blame themselves for what happened to them. Thoughts ruminate about what they could have done differently to have prevented it. When sexual molestation and rape are carried out by same sex individuals, more often than not, victims question their sexuality while secretly wrestling with conflicting thoughts like: "I must be homosexual"…"they must have seen something in me that indicates I am gay in order for them to have targeted me."

The first experience lie robs many of having a healthy sex life. That lie is, whatever your first sexual experience is, determines your sexuality. Victims are often affected in one or two ways: they become sexually promiscuous or experience sexual aversion (do not want to engage in sexual relationship at all). Victims of sexual molestation and/or rape become depressed and they question their self-value and self-worth, hence experiencing an identity crisis.

Marriage

Now we will look at marriage. Marriage is an exciting time in most people's lives. The coming together of two individuals into a single union is something coveted by most singles. Most people see the glory of marriage, but are never really aware of the work that goes into the preservation of marriage. After the honeymoon phase, marriage becomes very challenging for most. A friend of mine helped me see the fact that two people joining and becoming one is a very painful process, and the Bible is clear on that. According to Genesis, Scripture states, "Therefore shall a man leave his father and mother and cleave unto his wife and the two shall become one flesh." (2:24) Do you know that the word "cleave" has a direct implication that there will be the process of severing, being split, cut off, to be carved, and to penetrate making a way through something forcefully?[3]

An attempt to alleviate or at best lessen the pain of the process of cleaving creates a milieu in which it becomes easy for one or both people in the relationship to lose a sense of self-identity. This creates a crisis of the identity within the marriage. There should be a freedom to maintain individuality, uniqueness, and personality within the confines of the relationship; the person you were when your spouse fell in love with you should not be displaced but rather enhanced, made better, more aligned with the you that you are in Christ as you become Christ-like in the relationship. It should be that as spouses maintain their uniqueness in the relationship in their pursuit of God, they become by default what the other spouse needs; it is in this place that identity of both spouses' individualization and unification is achieved.

Divorce

Divorce, on the other hand, is a separation of the union. It is a breaking away. I like to liken a divorce to a death which I'm sure many can relate to this analogy. Most people have been impacted by divorce in some way—whether you've experienced your parents' divorce, your own divorce, or the divorce of someone close to you. Many have felt the pain of divorce directly or indirectly. I have witnessed and heard many stories of life after divorce. Many survivors of divorce have feelings of being lost and feeling out of sorts. They are no longer able to identify their "self." The question of *Who am I?* surfaces because their identity died in the relationship and/or at the point of divorce. Children surviving divorce tend to have a crisis of their own. After all that was considered normal becomes abnormal for children, no matter how dysfunctional prior, the identity suffers after divorce. Having to redefine things like family, relationships, and home can be disconcerting for children of divorce, no matter their age.

Empty-Nest Syndrome

The empty-nest syndrome is another cause of an identity crisis. When children leave home to go off to college, get married, or simply to live the single life, parents often become confused about who they are and their role in society. They often lose their identity because their identity has been defined and derived from their role of being a mother or a father; but who belongs to you is not who you are. Your role as a parent is not who you are, nor for that matter is it the entirety of your purpose in life. After spending years of overcommitting to your children and putting them before yourself and your marriage, the you that existed long before children gets buried overtime. Parents go through a process of having to rediscover a sense of self. Questions of Who am I? and Who is my spouse? Surface when experiencing an empty-nest identity crisis. Your identity is more than the sum total of your children.

Transitional Crisis

Now, let's look at a transitional crisis. Transitions can vary. You can be transitioning from one job to another. You can transition from work to unemployment. Going from working to unemployment can wreak havoc on the emotional state of a person. Worry and anxiety heighten as one searches for work and meets challenges during the search. Moving or relocating from a home or one state to another can pose a transitional crisis. Changing from one social or economic status to another can also cause a crisis of the identity. Transitions can bring on confusion about one's role in society. Having to reconnect and reestablish new relationships can be daunting. Trying to assert confidence in your uniqueness during transition is difficult. In most cases, people in this situation also go through a process of rediscovering themselves and their purpose in life all over again.

Severing of Friendships

Severing of friendships can have some of the same effects of divorce. Friendships take time to develop—in some cases, decades. When someone is close to you, that person becomes a part of you. Typically, friends share private information with one another that other people will never be privy to. There is intimacy and history in a friendship. When friendships are severed, feelings of anger, sadness, resentment, pain, and confusion arise. When a friendship ends that was bad for you, feelings of low self-esteem and depression may surface. One may find themselves having to heal and deal with mental and emotional crises that would have never existed if you had walked away from the relationship when abuse initially presented itself in the friendship.

Having closure is often helpful to the healing process, but most people are not fortunate enough to get closure. For many people, having friends provides a sense of identity and self-worth, but you are not who you are associated with. You should never base your identity on the friendships you have, but the friends you have should be drawn to the light of your identity. Like couples divorcing, the identity of an individual can get lost in the friendship. One then has to go through a process of discovering, *Who am I without my friends?* The best way to maintain a sense of self is to make Jesus Christ your best Friend. Then, when friends come and go, your identity will always remain complete and intact.

Midlife Crisis

Now, let's look at a midlife crisis. A midlife crisis occurs when what you have done in life is no longer working. Bewilderment sets in as men and women realize their life has not progressed in the manner they thought it would, or in the manner society has said that it should. Feelings of being overwhelmed, sadness, regret, and unhappiness can fester. People experiencing a midlife crisis feel they lack direction in life. The feeling of inadequacy then causes a crisis of the identity to erupt. If one fails to identify their identity and purpose at this stage in life, they will attempt to fill the void by turning to immediate gratification through extramarital affairs, overeating, overspending, or the like. Some may even attempt to fill the void by giving themselves to others and by overcommitting in relationships. You can get stuck here if you focus on the years you think you've wasted. You have to search with the Spirit of God's help for your purpose in life. Your purpose will provide you with the strategy you need to not only escape the midlife crisis, but will also provide a plan that will become the driving force to help you achieve your goals and dreams in life so you can reach your destiny.

Retirement

Last, but not least, we will look at retirement. Retirement can be both an exciting and terrifying time. So often, a career furnishes an identity for people, especially men. There is this misconception that what you do is who you are. You are not your profession. For many retirees, coming out of the workforce presents a new set of challenges and concerns. Numerous retirees do not have enough money for retirement and so they re-enter the workforce. Some feel like they are wasting away by not contributing to society, so they re-enter the workforce without taking the time to intentionally identify their purpose in life after retirement which creates more identity issues. The desire, concern, and/or fear of death heighten at this time in life as retirees realize that much of life is behind them. Discovering distinctiveness and purpose in this period of life can be achieved with an understanding of who you are in Christ Jesus.

There are so many other things that can bring about the onset of an identity crisis. For example, being in an environment of verbal, emotional, and physical abuse can create an identity crisis. Being neglected, disappointment in life, failure, sin issues, and a myriad of other issues can cause an identity crisis. I will talk more about these and their harmful influence on your identity later.

If you will review some of the things I previously mentioned that trigger an identity crisis, you will gather that it is possible to have more than one crisis at the same time. For example, it is very likely to have multiple crises when experiencing a divorce, transitioning to a new location, starting a new job, and having to establish all new relationships.

Can you imagine the emotional turmoil as one may desperately work to understand who they are, reconstruct a sense of self that is valued, and regain an active role in society with all these changes? This is overwhelming! If not careful, the crisis of the identity can leave you feeling hopeless and in despair. I would like to submit to you that no matter how diverse or unique an identity crisis is, all identity crises are the sole result of *one* root identity deficit. You will not only come to understand what that one major identity crisis is that is at the root of various other crises, but you will also discover how to overcome it!

Feelings Associated with An Identity Crisis

People experiencing an identity crisis are conflicted about aspects of their character and the internal conflict becomes a source of duress and disorientation. Feelings of unhappiness and insecurity, as well as thoughts of inadequacy, often plague the person during an identity crisis. When we cannot truthfully answer the questions, *Who am I?* and *What is my purpose?*, confusion sets in. Feelings of hopelessness come into play which are akin to depression. Depression is simply anger turned inward. Lacking identity creates self-hatred overtime. Thoughts like, *I am incapable of change, I'm not good enough,* or *I'm not worthy of love and acceptance* simmers. These thoughts are destructive in nature. If left unattended, they will boil over into a disastrous end.

Anger

Anger is another emotion that can be experienced during an identity crisis. Angry people tend to hold on to hurt and pain, and then explode. Anyone who stands in the path of an angry man is bound to become victim of his rage. Angry people tend to have a superiority complex where they have to dominate, control, and manipulate the people around them when things do not go the way they want them to go. Angry people are broken and just as confused as the next person about life. The search for identity and purpose is ambiguous and who can tolerate uncertainty without undesirable emotions materializing?

Inadequacy

I am sure some of these emotions are resonating with you. Perhaps you relate to and can even identify with some of these emotions as you attempt to discover who you are. Have you ever felt inadequate? Feelings of inadequacy will make you feel you are not good enough or that you do not measure up. Other mental disturbances like depression, low self-esteem, low self-worth, anxiety, PTSD, and codependency often perpetuate feelings of inadequacy creating a condition in which it is impossible for an individual to be successful, happy, or at peace. For many people, feelings of inadequacy are rooted in childhood experiences. On top of these, other undesirable events come along that make an immense contribution to feelings of inadequacy such as workplace nuisance, peer pressure, and bullying.

Those who experience feelings of inadequacy carry the sting from yesteryears into their future. As a child, they may have had close relatives who were abusive or overly critical. Many children with critical parents often experience harsh criticism, being controlled and compared to other's children, all of which contribute to feelings of inadequacy in childhood that is carried into adulthood. Adulthood presents many more challenges that nurture feelings of inadequacy; marriage and the workplace become some of the biggest challenges that breed these feelings. Having to work in a toxic work environment can also cause someone to feel that they are incompetent, thus fueling inadequacy. Traumatic experiences within the church have become of great detriment to many Christians, causing them to feel the brunt of inadequacy. Regrettably, there are many Christians who come to the house of God for help with feelings of inadequacy and other concerns—only to have their wounded souls further crushed by critical, judgmental saints. (And let me just say, this should not be among us!) People who suffer due to feelings of inadequacy may exhibit some of the following symptoms:

- Anxiety, particularly with regards to performance
- Heightened sensitivity and self-criticism
- Reluctance to accept or trust in the affections of others
- Feelings and thoughts of the inability to show affection to others
- Low self-worth
- Fear of failure
- Perceptions of rejection
- The inability to accept praise
- Feelings of powerlessness
- The disposition to conform or succumb to peer pressure[4]

All of these feelings associated with an identity crisis serve as a barrier to our ability to identify our individuality, uniqueness, personality, and purpose in life. When we spiral into a crisis of the identity, we often feel shame and embarrassment. The first thing we want to do is go into hiding. No one wants to feel exposed, vulnerable, or at risk for ridicule because there is a lack of identity where we don't know who we are or our purpose in life. The quick fix for such a dilemma often leads to the wearing of a mask.

Masked

The word personality is derived from the Latin word *persona*, which means mask.[5] The meaning of mask in ancient Latin does not take on the same connotations that it takes on in modern society. Historically, the Latin word mask was not a means of disguise, but rather, a true depiction of the personality and character of a person. Yet, in today's vernacular, a mask is understood to be what we put on to disguise ourselves.

But why do we wear masks? For some, it is purely with the intent to deceive and manipulate others. However, for most of us, the mask is a counterfeit protective barrier. Life is often met with pain, loss, bitter disappointments, confusion, trauma, and drama. We hide for fear of rejection. Thoughts like—*If people really knew who I really am, they would not like me*, or, *If only they knew what I struggle with, they would lose all respect for me and probably would not want to have anything to do with me*—start to become our default inner dialogue. The inner dialogue that is filled with negative thoughts creates fear of punishment, fear of rejection, or of betrayal of trust. It is thoughts like these that drive us into hiding. Feelings of shame, fear of failure, thoughts of insufficiency, not measuring up, not being good enough to be loved by others, or not meeting the approval of others will become pitfalls setup to ensnare you. Being vulnerable is scary when all your value and worth is resting on another person's appraisal of you!

All these negative feelings and erroneous thoughts are present in the midst of an identity crisis. They can easily be dismissed as mere expressions or indicators of a crisis, but they are so much more concerning, because they become strongholds—thought structures in your mind built on lies that gives Satan access to your life. He desires to keep you blind to these strongholds in an attempt to keep you in a defeated lifestyle, clutching for the mask.

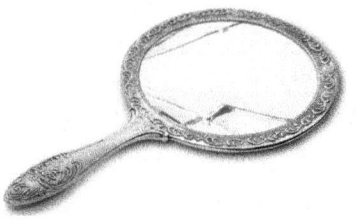

CHAPTER THREE

Understanding Strongholds

3
Understanding Strongholds

A stronghold originates in the mind. The apostle Paul penned in the book of 2 Corinthians that, "For though we walk in the flesh, we do not war after the flesh: For the weapons of our warfare are not carnal, but mighty through God to the pulling down of strongholds; Casting down imaginations and every high thing that exalteth itself against the knowledge of God, and bringing into captivity every thought to the obedience of Christ."(10:3-6) Notice Paul did not say that our weapons are for pulling down depression, anger, bitterness, resentment, doubt, fear, or inadequacy. All the issues I named are in fact strongholds, or rather the outcome of strongholds. So, there is a clear indication that the issues we have in our lives are just the offspring of a deeper seed planted beyond the reach of the surface.

The footholds Satan gains in our lives are first done through our thoughts. The scripture goes on with specific instruction: We are to cast down imaginations. Imaginations are mental images formed in the mind that are neither present nor experienced through any other sense like taste, touch, smell, sight, or hearing. Next, the scripture speaks of *casting down every high thing that exalts or lifts up itself against the knowledge of God*. The word "knowledge" implies information that is stored in the mind, or validated information that is available for the mind.

We will discuss this verse more in detail again in later chapters as we explore spiritual warfare, but the point I want to make here is that the enemy wants to gain a foothold that will lead to control of your thoughts, which will untimely lead to your demise in all other areas of your life. Satan forms these footholds in our thoughts by preying upon our emotional wounds and fears, insecurities and areas of weakness, and he exposes us to an erroneous narrative about our self that causes our mind to perceive reality through distorted, warped lens.

The more we begin to believe the erroneous narrative being fed to us, the more far-reaching the cancer spreads until every event and conversation becomes filtered through these faulty lens. This is a stronghold in the mind. More often than not, we are never the wiser; we fail to discern these strongholds are being formed because we do not take the time to challenge our thoughts or imaginations! Strongholds are the enemy's weapon of mass destruction. The formation of a stronghold can leave a person in bondage for years, and sadly many are bound by strongholds for a lifetime.

Inception of Strongholds

Satan starts forming strongholds as soon as we enter the world. Let's explore again the genesis of strongholds that begin in childhood. Everyone is born with innate survival instinct, and it was popular behaviorist, Walter Cannon, who introduced this concept to the field of behavior psychology in the 1920s. The theory of a fight-or-flight response to life stressors was introduced. I studied a course in college on counseling people who were alcoholics or drug abusers. The key bit of information I learned which has always stuck with me is that alcoholics drink in excess and drug addicts abuse drugs to self-medicate in order to mask their pain. Minus the substance abuse or drug abuse, all people do this in some way or another.

Most people self-medicate to mask their pain. This can be accomplished through acting out, fighting, bullying, isolating, being absorbed in relationships, being entertained, and being in denial; you name it. This process of fight-or-flight begins in childhood. It is a form of masking and the patterns extend throughout life. As children encounter pain from loved ones, they use two options to mitigate the pain. They either fight to mask the pain, or flee (withdraw, isolate) from the pain. Fighting provides some children with a means to control and overpower the painful stimuli. Other children flee to escape pain; avoiding pain altogether is desirable. Every time the child experiences pain, they choose their defense: fight or flee. These responses take on a vicious cycle throughout life until it becomes the default reaction to any external conflict.

While the response may prove to be effective, it will ultimately become a grievous task to continue, and this is where the formation of a stronghold takes shape. The fight-or-flight response at this point is not only used as an escape from pain, but leads to childish behavior well into adulthood. This self-centered reactionary kink of avoidance thinking and behavior becomes the compass by which people gauge how to go about getting the things they want in life. As stated by Robert McGee, "As pain spreads, most people continue their fight or flight responses...And frequently, when one response ceases to be effective, or when it begins to cause too much pain, the person finds a different response...Usually the new response is no better."[1] Deterioration begins as these responses lead to bigger strongholds like that of control and manipulation which are derived out of the fight response, and codependency which is derived from the flight response.

Classifying Strongholds

Let's break down the concept of strongholds a little more. As I have stated previously, strongholds are footholds in your life that the enemy has access to; they are extensions of thought patterns rooted in traumatic experiences that often occurred during childhood. Since it would take a tremendous amount of time to name all of the different types of strongholds, we will focus on the core few that are widespread and prevalent to the human experience.

Insecurity: Insecurity is the underpinning to many other issues like an inferiority complex and feelings of inadequacy, and it breeds anxiety and fear. Insecurity causes you to be deficient in self-confidence and lack self-worth. Insecure people have avoidant personalities where they flee conflict to alleviate pain. People that have an inferiority complex always feel they are less important and of less value than their counterparts, often bound by fear of being exposed or found out. The feelings of inadequacy cause people to feel and believe that they can never measure up to others and that others are better than they are.

Depression: Did you know that some of the greatest men and women in history experienced bouts of deep depression? Consider King David for one. He was known to be a man after God's own heart; however, he wrote in Psalms, "Why, my soul, are you downcast? Why so disturbed within me? Put your hope in God." (42:11) David knew what it was like to feel discouraged, disillusioned, and unhappy. Depression is another form of anger; anger turned inward.

Depression causes people to live with their past always in view. Focusing on past mistakes and failures will lead to feelings of regret, which is inner anger stemming from past disappointments over poor choices made. Depression brings on feelings of hopelessness, shame, and embarrassment, which draws people into isolation and losing interest in life.

Depression is nothing to be ashamed of. Do you know that more than 350 million people worldwide experience it? And that is just what is reported. It is the leading cause of disability.₂ Depression leads to despair and self-pity. In severe cases, if left unaddressed, depression can lead to thoughts of suicide. (If this describes you, please get help.) When we mask depression, it becomes a stronghold. The symptoms of depression are rooted in believing a lie about yourself, others, and your circumstances. Masking depression and failing to utilize the weapons of our warfare by pulling down these strongholds (lies and wrong thinking) says to God and your adversary, "I believe these lies." Satan will see that you are not willing to do the work of pulling down unconstructive imaginations and he will prey upon you, using your unwillingness or ignorance to the fact that you can end your depression and use it to wreak havoc in your life time after time.

Bitterness: Bitterness is a silent killer which easily goes undetected. Other emotions or strongholds linked to bitterness may be detected long before bitterness itself. Feelings like anger, resentment, and unforgiveness will rise to the surface long before bitterness. Bitterness is the persistence of anger, resentment, and unforgiveness that brews over a long period of time. These mounting feelings often lead to violent acts that erupt in the heat of the moment. People with bitterness are likely to assault others. In some cases, the assault birthed from deep-seated bitterness can be severe, such as murder or suicide.

Pride: Pride is undue self-importance, arrogance, feeling of superiority over others. When one feels he's better than another person, it is pride. When one places his or her needs above the needs of another, it is pride. Another form of pride is selfishness and self-centeredness which will produce thoughts of superiority and entitlement. People mask pride with self-confidence when they display their looks, gifts, and accomplishment above others—this is vainglory. Seeking vainglory and being self-righteous is another form of pride that often plagues religious people. Since religion is based on good works, people fall prey to pride when they have a high regard for their own moral performance rather than realizing that apart from Christ we are all flawed.

Addictions: Addictions are commonly understood in popular culture. One can be addicted to nicotine, alcohol, or drugs. However, most fail to identify other forms of addiction. There are addictions to food, sex, pornography, and in today's society there are mounting addictions like social media, television, fame, shopping, spending—you name it. As I have shared with you, addicts abuse their drug of choice in order to self-medicate, which gives them the illusion that they are escaping pain, failures, disappointment, and regrets. An addiction is a compulsive dependence on a substance, thing, or activity to alter mood.$_4$ Almost anything can be used to help numb the pain and stabilize a mood even if it provides temporary relief, which all addictions do. So, now we understand that addictions are outgrowths or symptoms of strongholds, which are initiated in the mind.

Recapping Strongholds

Strongholds are mental prisons and they vary in their form and strength. Deceit, doubt, fear, rebellion, occult engagement, sexual impurity, and many others are all forms of strongholds Satan uses to keep us enslaved.$_3$ Strongholds dominate lives; they are destructive and require intentional exploration with often intense focus and diligence to break free from them. Strongholds are often rooted in childhood stemming from emotionally wounding events which instilled a reactionary, trauma-based mode of living where everything is filtered through the lens of a fight-or-flight threat—depriving one of living a freedom-centered life of love, joy, and peace. As we continue this journey together, you will learn truths in this book that will help you dismantle the strongholds in your life. You do not have to be prisoner to your strongholds!

Coping with Strongholds

Strongholds are mental roadblocks that keep us deceived and believing things that are not advantageous to our welfare. Strongholds become destructive to our mental, emotional, social, and spiritual health. We can categorize strongholds into two distinct models: nonmaterial and material. Nonmaterial strongholds are those that are of the ideology, constructed dogma, imagination(s), internal codes, and personal belief systems.

Material strongholds manifest themselves behaviorally and are compulsive behaviors that one cannot stop nor change. Material strongholds are manifestation of the nonmaterial strongholds themselves. This is where the stronghold(s) move(s) beyond your thoughts to a more expressive form through your emotions and your actions. Note that any material stronghold is first conceived in the mind; it is primarily nonmaterial.

Strongholds are patterns that have developed over a period of time. The genesis of these strongholds began in childhood. These acquired patterns exist at present because you did not deal with them when they arose. If you want to get to the root of your stronghold(s)—and you should if you desire to be free of them—then you must be willing to visit the memories of childhood. This can be a very painful method so you cannot be passive about this process. I don't want you to survive because you have developed a coping mechanism; I want you to live free from your stronghold. Surviving is all well and good, but really, what good is just surviving in life? Confront your past. I am not suggesting you visit painful memories and live in them, but what I am saying is that you have to confront them. Be honest with yourself that they exist, then forgive. Forgive the people who were a part of helping to create the strongholds and forgive yourself for holding onto them and for believing in a lie.

I address the concept of coping mechanisms because I have seen them at work in the lives of so many people I encounter. I have also erroneously adopted coping mechanisms to cope with the vicissitudes of life, so I get it. Coping mechanisms are just another term or way to better understand strongholds. They are usually symptoms of much deeper issues. Changing maladaptive behavior is important for mental wholeness and freedom. However, changing actual coping skills can be superficial—meaning you only deal with what is on the surface. Surface maintenance is usually what most people do because it is the area that people see. The notion of confronting coping mechanisms is a noble thought, but ultimately, it will lead to failure. Why failure? Because surface maintenance is simply behavior modification and that does not last. Rather, what is needed is an experience of a heart transformation on the inside. This is what is paramount in order to gain permanent and lasting freedom from strongholds.

Coping Mechanisms

As a child, when faced with painful events, we often looked for ways to escape or ways to create a more desirable outcome. In childhood, when your resolve did not prove effective you then began developing coping mechanisms, commonly called defense mechanisms. Coping mechanisms from a child's perspective are not bad in and of themselves. In fact, as children have to develop ways to cope and remain resilient in the face of life fluctuations, many who do develop coping mechanisms can be seen as innovative, resilient, and effective. Problems emerge when we carry these same defense/coping mechanisms into adulthood. The way you saw and dealt with life in your adolescent years will not be effective in adulthood. Defense mechanisms are patterns used to deal with conflict and pain like masking and addictions. They are developed in childhood for resolution and preservation purposes. They become a rational and practical response for the child who is by nature weak and inferior to those surrounding him. Children have a limited ability to reason rationally. Unaware of their limitations, they make the most rational choice that minimizes pain and creates a milieu in which they can get their needs met. What was effective in childhood becomes a serious impediment in adulthood.

While this is not a book about psychology in itself, I would like to denote that certain theories discussed in portions of this book illustrate key concepts to aid you in an understanding of psychology terminology and theories that highlight the causality of identity crisis. And to that end, let's look at Sigmund Freud. Freud was a world-renowned psychoanalysis. His classical theories assert the idea that all of humanity's problems are rooted in the unconscious—meaning, problems reside in that region of the human psyche that is unknown to him. Freud believed that everyone suffering from mental and emotional trauma could be healed by having a cathartic experience through a process that would make the unaware aware by unearthing repressed thoughts.

Freud was a pioneer in the field of psychology. His theories were fundamental to the groundwork of psychology. While some of his theories were and are controversial, his profound contributions cannot be discounted. Freud managed to submit to the world the notion of coping and defense mechanisms that are effective and valid for many today. As we have begun to address the premise of defense mechanisms, I think it would be helpful for you to see a list of some and note which may apply to you. This is important in helping you become aware of any coping skills you have adopted and you will later see how they may have become an ineffective means of dealing with life in adulthood. Below are some examples of coping mechanisms:

- Rationalization—excuses given to justify a wrong behavior
- Projection—attempts to disown wrong behavior or thoughts by blaming others
- Introjections (opposite of projection)—taking the thoughts and actions of others inward, imprinting them to self
- Isolation—suppressed memories or separating emotions where they forget or talk about a traumatic event without emotion
- Identification—attaching the emotions, actions, thoughts of someone else to yourself; taking on the identity of another
- Displacement—taking feeling and/or action out on an innocent person
- Repression—hiding traumatic event(s), emotions, pain, grief, and/or impulses deep inside (done unconsciously)
- Suppression—hiding trauma, pain, grief, threatening emotions, and impulses deep inside (done consciously)

- Denial—treating grief, traumatic events, threatening emotions and unpleasant facts as if they do not exist₅

This list is just a few of the defense mechanisms/strongholds. After reading them you probably can identify where you may have used them or know someone who uses them to cope with life. Suppression is the only one in the list that is done consciously. Almost all defense mechanisms are done unconsciously. That means you are not aware when you are using defense mechanisms as a means of coping--a sure way Satan keeps you deceived. Keep in mind that this list of defense mechanisms is actually redefined strongholds, just as the list under feelings of inadequacy is redefined strongholds. The thing with defense mechanisms and strongholds is that they tend to distort and falsify your perceptions, which in turn, alter your reality.

Mask or Move On?

The most effective way to alleviate harmful coping patterns is to discover the root of the matter and confront it. You need to see the core of the distorted self before you can renew and become your true self. In other words, you have to know you have a problem (a stronghold), then you have to desire change before changing any stronghold. The habits and patterns learned in childhood become maladaptive behaviors in adulthood. Attacking the core issues will allow you to see undesirable childhood patterns dissipate over time and you will find your identity coming into form.

You may wonder just how many people are impacted by feelings of inadequacy and other strongholds. The truth is that at some point or another we all experience feelings of inadequacy and everyone has some sort of mental stronghold. Rather than get help to be free from strongholds and various thoughts of inadequacy, people tend to shrink further in hiding forever, wearing a mask. The problem with wearing a mask is that after you wear it for so long, the uneasiness of concealing yourself becomes a grievous task. You wear the mask at the expense of actually getting to know your real self, the person you were created to be. Any threat that comes in opposition to you understanding your true identity will thrust you into a crisis of the identity. Your identity crisis will give place to darkness, and in that darkness, any and all occasion of stumbling will take place. You begin to realize that maintaining the mask is hard work. Yet, I submit to you that discarding your mask can be just as challenging, but far more rewarding! The question then comes, do you want to hang on to the mask, or are you ready to let it go?

CHAPTER FOUR

The Lazarus Effect

4
The Lazarus Effect

One night, I was in bed and I felt the gentleness of the Spirit of God. So I laid there for a moment and basked in His presence. I told the Spirit of God, "You can speak to me while I lay here." Yes, I was being lazy. I didn't want to get out of bed, and go to another room to get in the presence of God. Shameful, right? But it's the truth. I felt like, *Lord, I sense you are here and all, let me continue here in your presence. Speak to me.* Well, the presence of the Lord gently went away…and I lay there thinking, Wait a minute, what if I miss out on something? What if He wants to tell me something? I knew if I didn't get up I was going to miss out on something.

So, I got up to pray and read my Bible in the guest room like I usually do. Then I felt the need to read the story of God raising Lazarus from the dead. Still being a bit lazy, I thought, *Why do I need to read this story when I have read it and heard it so many times before?* Reluctantly, I began reading a translation online that I do not usually read, and I noticed the interpretation being a bit different from that which I had read in the King James Version. As a curious being, I wanted to check the facts, as if the experts may have made a mistake.

Now I was starting to wake up from my laziness and really search the scriptures. After reading the story a second time through, I began to ask the Lord questions about the text. Oddly enough, I was starting to see something there I had not seen before. I began to see the crisis within humanity. I could see that God's interjection with humanity was a central theme within the account of Jesus' resurrection of Lazarus. The concept that humanity's identity was in question was taking shape before my eyes. Lazarus serves as a symbol of what God can do for those in search of identity.

An Overview of Jesus Raising Lazarus

The story is familiar for many Christians, but I won't take it for granted that you know it. Lazarus was the brother of Martha and Mary. Jesus loved them all and was friends with this family. They lived in Bethany and Jesus was away with His disciples when He received the message sent to Him from Martha, Lazarus' sister, that Lazarus was sick and dying. When Jesus received the message, He was confident that Lazarus' end would not be death; yet, instead of going to see His friend He stayed where they were for two more days. After those two days, Jesus said to His disciples, "Let us go back to Judea."

His disciples immediately protested, "Why do you want to go back to Judea?" They conferred that the last time they were in Judea the Jews wanted to kill Jesus; they wanted to stone him! As I continued reading, I thought Jesus gave the strangest response to their argument. He said, *"Are there not twelve hours in the day? If any man walk in the day, he stumbleth not, because he seeth the light of this world. But if a man walk in the night, he stumbleth, because there is no light in him."* (John 11:9-10) He then told His disciples that Lazarus was sleeping and that He was going to wake Lazarus up. While His disciples were thinking Lazarus was sleeping a natural sleep, they thought he would wake up himself and recover from his sickness over time, but Jesus had to inform them that Lazarus was, in fact, dead.

So the disciples accompanied Jesus to wake Lazarus. Upon Jesus' arrival, He found that Lazarus had been dead for four days, buried in a tomb. When Martha heard Jesus was coming, she went to meet him. When she arrived, she told Jesus," If you were here, my brother would not have died." Martha also told Jesus that if He asked His Father for something, He would do it for him, even in the face of Lazarus' death. Jesus knew within himself that the Father was going to raise Lazarus from the dead. He told Martha that Lazarus would rise again. Of course, Martha thought Jesus was referring to the last days when all the saints of God will rise to be with the Lord on high. Jesus corrected her and comforted her by saying, "I am the resurrection and the life." (John 11:25) Jesus simply wanted her to believe, and she would see this miracle. The once-busy Martha had great faith that Jesus was the Son of God and could do what He said.

After Martha's encounter, she went back and told her sister Mary that Jesus was calling for her. When Mary heard Jesus sent for her, she left immediately, and so did the Jews who were visiting to comfort Mary and Martha. They thought she was going to the tomb to grieve more so they planned to accompany her that they may be of comfort, only to find she was going to meet Jesus. Mary cried out to Jesus, "If you had been here, he would not have died!" Mary sobbed and so did the Jews. Jesus saw their sorrow and *He wept*.

Jesus made His way to the tomb where Lazarus was laid to rest and requested they remove the stone that covered the tomb. Martha told Jesus that Lazarus had been dead for four days, and that his body would have a terrible stench. Jesus reminded her that if she'd just believe on Him, she would see the glory of God. So, they removed the stone. Jesus then cried with a loud voice, "Lazarus, come forth!" And Lazarus came forth out the tomb...**his hands and feet were bound with strips of burial linens, and his face was covered with a burial napkin.** Jesus commanded them to, "Loose him and let him go!"

God and Humanity, the Central Theme

Admittedly, I have read this several times and heard it preached throughout the course of many years, but I did not know what other revelations were hidden in the text. I began to contemplate why Jesus waited **two whole days** before He went to see Lazarus. Another question came to mind was why did John make it a point to note that Lazarus had been dead **four days** by the time Jesus had arrived to see him? Why did Jesus cry? Why was it important to note "Jesus wept"? I began to research the meaning of the numbers **two** and **four,** as they would have been written originally in the Hebrew and Greek text. My research revealed that the number **two** means *separation or union,* and *comparison and contrast.* The number **two** also means *a verification of facts by witness.*[1] Both historically and biblically, it was legally and judicially required and customary for there to be at least **two** witnesses or more in order to convict someone of a crime or sin. Likewise, there had to be **two** or more people to corroborate and authenticate truth. Even Jesus told the Pharisees that, as it was written in the law, the testimony of two men was necessary to be considered truth. (John 8:17) Jesus waited **two** days after hearing His friend was dying, even though He knew that He would raise Lazarus from the dead. The Father would resurrect Lazarus through Him so that those who looked on would bear witness and see that Jesus was truly the Son of God, sent by God to redeem sinful men. This was the Father's intent; this was Jesus' purpose in life.

When Jesus told His disciples that Lazarus was dead, He also said, "I am glad for your sakes that I was not there, to the intent ye may believe." (John 11:15) Jesus also prayed, "Father, I thank thee that thou has heard me. And I know that thou hearest me always; but because of the people which standby I said it, that they may believe that thou hast sent me." (John 11:41-42) The important truth here is that Jesus waited **two days** to go to Bethany to see Lazarus because He wanted there to be a verification of the truth by two or more witnesses proving that He was the Son of God sent to be the light of the world; a concept we will explore in the next section. God legally established truth in the earth that would be revolutionary for humanity.

Dividing the Light from the Dark

As I continued to ponder the scriptures, I wondered why it was important to note in the word of God the **four days** Lazarus was dead before Jesus would see about him? According to the Bible Study Site, the number four has the following meaning:

> The number 4 derives its meaning from creation. On the fourth day of what is called "creation week" God completed the material universe. On this day He brought into existence our sun, moon, and all the stars (Genesis 1:14-19). Their purpose was not only to give off light, but also to divide the day from the night on earth, thus becoming a basic demarcation of time. They were also made to be a type of signal that would mark off the days, years, and seasons. [2]

If we go back to the strange statement Jesus made to His disciples when they rebutted His decision to go back into Judea for fear that the Jews would kill Jesus, Jesus addresses their concern with this statement, *"Are there not twelve hours in the day?"* (John 11:9) "He stumbleth not, because he seeth the light of this world. But if a man walk in the night, he stumbleth, because there is no light in him." (John 11: 9-10) With this statement Jesus informed His disciples that He would awake Lazarus and then He explained Lazarus was, in fact, dead. Now let's make the connection of Jesus' response to His disciples, the miracle He did in raising Lazarus from the dead, and why Jesus wept.

Making the Connection

Early on in the book of John, Jesus said to the Pharisees, "I am the light of the world: He that followeth me shall not walk in darkness, but shall have the light of life." (John 8:12) When Jesus raised Lazarus from the dead, He was revealing to those who looked on as witnesses that He was sent by God the Father and He was truly the Son of God. Not only that, *He revealed the truth that He was the way, the truth, and the life.* (John 14:6) If any man would dare to believe on Jesus, he would not only have eternal life, but would also be able to live a life of freedom and a life of abundance. Those who believe on Jesus will be empowered to live a life free from sin and any occasion of stumbling because he would have the light of the Son of God to illuminate his path all the days of his life. Jesus is the only one who can remove darkness with light because He is light. You don't have to go through life stumbling in darkness and faltering at every turn. Jesus, your light, will be a lamp unto your feet and a light on your path all the days of your life. Just let Him!

Final Analysis

The last point I want to convey to you from this wonderful story of the resurrection of Lazarus is that the shortest sentence in the Bible noting the fact that "Jesus wept" is a window into the heart of God. While many teachings say Jesus was touched with empathy by their sorrow at the loss of their loved one, He wept. Teachings also say that Jesus wept because He loved Lazarus; Lazarus was His friend. I believe all of this to be true, but let me submit to you the notion that Jesus also wept for another reason. While mourning the death of Lazarus He looked out and saw Mary and others whom He loved in emotional anguish. Jesus saw their true condition. Man was never intended to die nor experience the intense pain associated with loss. More so, Jesus wept because He knew that humanity had lost their identity; humanity was in darkness, completely devoid of light and truth. This, my dear friends, is why Jesus wept. Jesus rising Lazarus would be His opportunity to establish truth that He was the Son of God. His resurrection of Lazarus was His opportunity to divide the darkness (every occasion of stumbling and ignorance of the truth) from the light (the knowledge of the truth) to reveal that He was Jesus Christ the Son of God, Savior of humanity.

According to the Bible Study Tool through Crosswalk.com, the Hebrew meaning for Lazarus is "God has help."[3] God the Father has sent the help you need in this life through His Son Jesus Christ. When Lazarus did come forth, he was bound by the hands and feet. His head was also covered with a burial napkin. Jesus said, "Loose him and let him go!" This is a picture of the power unto salvation whereby men would be unchained, freed, and their blinders removed so that they might walk in the light and live in the light of their true identity, which is in the Son of God.

I felt strongly to share this message with you because I desire that you know truth and experience freedom. As you move on throughout this book, it is my prayer that the Spirit of God will divide the darkness from the light in your life. Jesus saw humanity's lack of identity. Having a flawed sense of self, lacking an identity, is equivalent to living in darkness. When you come to know whose you are, who you are, and your purpose in life, light shines! You shine! I pray that you realize your true identity. May you no longer walk in darkness or in an unawareness of the reality of your true self. With Christ, I believe that you will transcend the crisis that comes in darkness through the light of understanding your identity. The night is far spent; the rays of the sun are shining, heralding the dawn. Now may you walk in the light of Son of God forever!

SECTION TWO

Three Roadblocks to Discovering Your Identity

CHAPTER FIVE

Satan: Your Adversary

5
Satan: Your Adversary

We wrestle with conflict daily, at times, moment-by-moment. Often we fail to realize that we have a real adversary at the root of all our conflict. Satan, the world, other people, and the flesh are all opposing forces we have to deal with throughout the course of life. At various stages all three opposing forces will create roadblocks on one's journey to self-discovery. We will talk more about the roadblocks the world and the flesh present in the following chapters. This chapter will focus on Satan as the primary roadblock to discovering your true identity.

Satan and his forces are in complete opposition to God and God's kingdom. Satan is the ruler of the kingdom of darkness. We are surrounded by a cloud of witnesses beyond this natural realm where the kingdom of darkness is at constant odds with the kingdom of heaven. These spiritual conflicts between two opposing kingdoms impact lives in the natural realm (in the earth). The kingdom of heaven has made great advances from the onset of Jesus' ministry even till now, but suffers violence at the hands of the kingdom of darkness. (Matthew 11:12) We can reverse the assault of the wicked one, Satan, by becoming violent in our pursuit of the kingdom of heaven.

To better understand me, let's look at the word violent from the Greek perspective, it means to become eager and on fire in our pursuit of the kingdom of heaven as to even thrust ourselves into it. Those who become vigorous in their pursuit of God, those who become conscious and strong spiritually, can disarm the kingdom of darkness. In doing so, they become empowered by the Spirit of God to live out the destiny God has for them.

I find that many people live as if the kingdom of darkness does not exist. Sadly enough, many do not believe in the presence of evil actively at work in the world. I'm not here to convince you that Satan is real. However, I would like to take a moment to discuss our adversary. It is important to shed light and provide insight and soberness concerning the intent and schemes of the enemy. Being aware of Satan's guises will better equip you to deal with conflicts that arise from the kingdom of darkness. Dismantling stumbling blocks Satan places in your path will keep you in the light, free from any impediments on your journey to realizing your identity.

Accuser of the Brethren

The Bible calls Satan "the accuser of the brethren."(Revelation 12:10) Accuser in the Greek is *kategoros*.[1] Accusers are basically informers, prosecutors, rats, and tattletales. This is exactly what Satan does to the children of God day and night. He actively seeks to bring accusations against God's people with the sole intent to prevent them from living their destinies. While doing so, Satan deceives us by causing us to feel and believe we are condemned. Proof of his accusations can be felt in your personal life as you experience real feelings of guilt and shame. Satan knows that if he can get you to feel guilt and shame, he can thwart the plan of God for your life. This lie will cause you to never fully come to an understanding of who you are in Christ which, in turn, prevents you from achieving your destiny.

Satan and his forces are hateful and void of any capacity to love. He will do whatever it takes to devour you. John 10:10 says, "The thief cometh not but for to steal, and to kill, and to destroy." Remember how Jesus wept because He saw the true state of humanity. Humanity had lost their identity. This was the work of Satan from the beginning, and he persists in committing the crime of identity theft. As Satan steals identities, he takes with him the ability for you to know your true value, he defrauds you of an opportunity to identify your purpose in life, and destroys any chance of you living out your destiny. He fights smart but dirty.

Satan, Your Adversary

Satan is also addressed in scriptures as an adversary. Adversary in the Greek is translated *antikdikos*. According to the New Testament Greek Lexicon, adversary means "an opponent in a suit of law, an enemy".[2] Satan draws attention to your weaknesses and your shortcomings. He is continuously before God attempting to prosecute believers in the courtroom of heaven. Satan uses allegations of sin as a means to justify his rule on earth, and the power and authority he receives each time humanity sins.

In every attempt to sustain the kingdom of darkness, Satan and his followers keep God's people ignorant of the truth. Satan desires that all men live in and abide in darkness. Our adversary has often succeeded at robbing the people of God of the things that rightfully belong to them in Christ. The adversary employs his secret weapon of deception to blind God's people of the treasure they are and the wealth they have in Christ Jesus. Peter urges believers to "be sober, be vigilant; because your adversary the devil, as a roaring lion, walketh about, seeking whom he may devour." (1 Peter 5:8) It is critical to be conscious of the schemes of the enemy so that he does not outsmart us. (2 Corinthians 2:11 NLT)

The fact is, Satan's devices have been known for centuries, but to those who are deceived, it stays a secret. Simply put, when you're deceived, you don't know you are deceived. Satan carries out his tactics of deception through lies, manipulation, and destruction through various means of temptation with the intent to keep the deceived in the dark. Temptations are hooks; they are agents used to lure believers into sin. Satan is clever at enticing you to draw you away in sin. Once you sin, Satan has a foothold in your life whereby he will come in and wreak havoc.

As long as Satan's influence goes unnoticed and he is believed to be nonexistent, he wins. Those who do not believe he exists will never come to realize that Satan's influence of spiritual darkness is at the root of all their problems. The unbelieving will continue to wrestle with identity and live in discontentment with themselves, as well as experience conflict with others, all the while failing to ascertain the real enemy. Paul writes to the church of Ephesians,

> For we are not wrestling with flesh and blood (contending only with physical opponents), but against the despotisms, against the powers, against (the master spirits who are) the world rulers of this present darkness, against the spiritual forces of wickedness in the heavenly (supernatural) sphere. (Ephesians 6:12 AMP)

Satan is busy at work trying to keep the world in darkness and trying to prevent the world from ever coming to know the truth of the gospel. The enemy wishes to pervert the influence and impact the saints have in the world through annihilating their testimonies. Being armed with this knowledge is fundamental to instruction on how to overpower the enemy. Before we discuss how to overcome Satan and the kingdom of darkness, we must be aware of his strategies for defeating us. You can never hope to defeat your opponent if you do not know your opponent, his strengths, and his weaknesses. I can assure you that Satan knows your strengths and your weaknesses, and you cannot defeat him apart from the authority of the Lord Jesus Christ and the power of the Holy Spirit.

Spiritual Displacement

Spiritual displacement is where you are moved from one spiritual state to another. In Christ there is no condemnation, no guilt nor shame, because of our right standing with God through Jesus Christ. Satan will deliberately deceive and manipulate you with the intent to move you to a state that is filled with guilt, shame, and condemnation. Satan uses various forms of temptation to cause Christians to be drawn away from God to a state that will promote failures in life. In the account of Jesus' temptation in the wilderness, we see where Satan tried to use his weapons of doubt and deception. He told Jesus, "If you are the Son of God, turn these stones into bread." (Matthew 4:3) The "if" was an implication that He might be the Son of God that He professed to be, or He might not be the Son of God. If Satan would have caused Jesus to doubt Himself, His identity, and His relationship to the Father, he would have defeated Jesus.

Jesus' response was, "Man does not live by bread alone, but by every word that proceeds out the mouth of God." (Matthew 4:4) After leading Jesus to the highest point in Jerusalem, Satan said, "If you are the son of God, cast yourself down . . . Surely, God will give His angels charge over you to keep you from dying or even dashing your foot against a stone." Satan tried to deceive Jesus by shrewdly challenging Him with the very Word of God, yet his deception did not work because Jesus' reply was that we are not to tempt the Lord our God. (Matthew 4:5-7) Satan's strategy is to place roadblocks in the lives of believers with the intent of spiritual displacement—preventing them from gaining awareness of their true identity.

Anytime Satan moves your spiritual state to one of doubt, fear, and condemnation, he has prevailed at displacement. He will have succeeded at getting you to move from your position of righteousness in Christ to one of guilt, shame, and/or condemnation. This one tactic is one of the most fundamental strategies in the kingdom of darkness. Satan uses spiritual blindness, denial, and spiritual displacement to advance his rule and authority.

A Look at Adam and Eve

If we look at the narrative of the fall of Adam and Eve, we see these tactics at play. After eating from the tree that was in the midst of the garden, which God had commanded them not to eat, they realized they were naked. They became fearful and ashamed, and so they covered themselves with fig leaves to cover their nakedness. They attempted to hide from God. Now, we know that they were never actually hidden from God, but because God desires communion and relationship with us, He inquired of Adam, "Where are you?" (Genesis 3:9 AMP) God asked whether he had eaten of the tree which he was commanded not to eat of (the tree of the knowledge of good and evil). Adam denied that he had done so while trying to place blame on Eve. The serpent had deceived Eve and she had eaten the fruit. Eve then managed to convince her husband, Adam, to partake of that which God told them not to eat.

Through the spiritual darkness cast by Satan, the once-wise Adam was unable to discern the truth. Once in darkness, imprudence perpetuates. As Adam went on to blame Eve for his sin, we can glean from this that anytime Satan can get you to deny the part you played in choosing to sin, and to place blame on another, he wins. And by doing so, he underhandedly steals your power and authority to live life as God intended you to live.

The consequences of Adam's sin caused him and Eve to be exiled from the Garden of Eden and the presence of God. (Genesis 3:19) Adam lost his privilege to live in the Garden of Eden where his work was pleasant, and he didn't have to labor through toil and sweat. Adam and Eve lost their position, influence, and impact. They also lost their power and authority in the world as a result of their choice to believe the serpent's lie that God was holding out on them. Satan bamboozled them into believing that everything God gave them, including perfect communion and relationship with Himself, was not good enough—the lie that they needed more. Adam and Eve lost the best part of themselves: their true identity. This great loss cost Adam his relationship with God. Adam had once communicated freely and peacefully with God. As a result of the deception and sin, this privilege with the Creator was no more.

Satan managed to cause Adam's relationship with God to be estranged through spiritual displacement. All of humanity would experience an estranged relationship with God from this point on, apart from Christ. With the fall of Adam, before the coming of Jesus Christ, humanity was distant and afar off from God and there was hostility between God and man—until Jesus came to reconcile us back to the Father.

Final Word

Satan's aim is always to place roadblocks in your path to cause you to stumble. He desires to draw you away, hindering your relationship with God. He knows he cannot keep you from heaven, but he can keep you from experiencing God's best for your life this side of heaven. He is working endlessly to keep you from your destiny and will succeed if he keeps you blind to the truth concerning your identity. Satan's agenda is to tempt you to sin and to bring accusations against you so he can devour you. Satan will use feelings of guilt, shame, and condemnation to do so. He will employ any means to prevent you from discovering your true identity because he knows that when you discover your identity you will absolutely unlock the abundant life Christ died for you to have!

CHAPTER SIX

The World:
The Celestial Collision

6
The World: The Celestial Collision

We all are exceptional beings created by God for a unique purpose. When purpose is found, our lives become enriched. How you characterize your identity will define your purpose in life, and your purpose will provide you with the trajectory you need to reach your destiny. Achieving your purpose in life creates lifelong fulfillment. Your purpose cannot be excavated until you have an accurate description and understanding of your identity. Obtaining an accurate knowledge of your identity can be foiled by the world's influences. Too often we are unaware of the impact the world has on our ability to see our true selves. We see shadows, mere illusions of our true identity. We become unsuspecting people who are unable to ascertain the gravity of the world's pull, living as if the kingdom of darkness is nonexistent within the world. We unconsciously feel at home in the world, then one with the world. At this point, we become ill-equipped to oppose the world's influences because we are oblivious to its continual, subtle sway.

Some of you may get exactly what I am saying, but I will break down the concept of the world a little more from a biblical perspective so you can clearly understand how *the world* can become a roadblock on the path to the discovery of your identity. The Bible talks about "the world" and how we are to view and interact with it based on three different concepts. Determining how the world influences your world will allow you to see its persuasiveness in your daily life. From a basic understanding, the world is understood to be the physical universe, the concrete earth, and all that is created/materialized within the earth. However, we will focus on the two concepts of "the world" that are relevant to living out your life.

The World Equivalent to Humanity

A well-known verse in John states, "For God so loved the world that he gave his only begotten Son that whosoever believes in him shall not perish but have everlasting life." (John 3:16) Here, we see *the world* being discussed within the context of humanity. God loves mankind: His creation. We are to mirror God in His love for humanity. Jesus told His disciples that the world would know we are His disciples by our love for one another. (John 13:25) Surely, He was telling the disciples to love all who are His, but this love was to extend beyond that to include unbelievers, which encompasses the entire world—humanity.

The story of the Good Samaritan highlights the call to love that we have as believers. It's important to realize that historically, it was unlawful and uncustomary for Jewish people to mix with other ethnic groups because of the idol worship carried out in other nations in the Old Testament. A lawyer, trying to test Jesus, told Him of the Mosaic Law to love God above all else, and to love your neighbor as yourself—being well aware that mixing with other ethnic groups was considered wrong. All other ethnic groups were considered Gentiles, or heathens.

To illustrate, Jesus tells the story of a man going down to Jericho from Jerusalem who was robbed by thieves and left for dead. A priest passed him by, as well as a Levite. Yet the priest, who was then a pillar of society and revered as holy, was unconcerned and did not help the wounded man. The Levite, being part of the nation that was chosen by God (Israel), also passed by, unconcerned for the life of the man. Then a Samaritan, a man who had no relevance and was not equivalent to the status of the priest nor the Levite, stopped to help this stranger in need.

As Jesus completed the story, He asked the lawyer, "Which is the neighbor to him that fell among thieves?" I can imagine the silly look on the lawyer's face when he had to state the obvious in saying, "The one that showed mercy." (Luke 10:25-37) Jesus' reply was for him to go and do likewise. The love we should have for the world involves our love for humanity. This love extends beyond geographical location, gender, race, or socioeconomic status. We are to freely love all as we are freely loved by God.

The World As It Relates to Identity

Worldliness is another biblical concept that we must be beware of as it relates to our lives and our identity. We identify ourselves based on the standards we observe in the world and by our experiences in the world. What we are acquainted with and lust after, we become. We then believe that our associations are accurate depictions of who we are. Who we think we should be becomes distorted as we view ourselves through the lens of society.

Our surroundings play an important part in defining who we are. And this is why we must be aware of our environment and intentionally create a milieu that is conducive to our spiritual well-being. There are things you cannot change in your environment and that goes without saying, but there are modifications you can make. For example, you can listen to preachers who teach the true word of God; you can nourish your spirit by listening to praise and worship music; you can spend at least five minutes a day praying. Getting alone in a quiet place is very important; even Jesus removed himself from the crowds in order to have a personal quiet time of prayer with the Father. It is important to disconnect with the world on occasion. Pulling away from the world—your surroundings—and spending time with God can alter the power of influence the world typically has on us.

The World As It Relates to the Flesh

Let's continue to look at this concept of the world in light of the influential worldly-fleshly characteristics of lust, anger, bitterness, selfishness, philosophies of men, and the culture at large. We can continue an endless list of worldly things. The world has a system in which it operates. We are told in 1 John not to love the world or the things that are in the world. If we love the world, then the love of our heavenly Father is not in us.(1 John 2:15-17) The "love of the world" here is not referring to people, *but to the world's system and its values that are at odds with God's values.* In essence, "the world" is a godless society. The values of the world will inevitably serve as roadblocks to discovering your true identity because they are the antithesis of godly values. The world we live in is driven by vain philosophies like hedonism, materialism, egoism, and individualism.

Hedonism and Materialism

Let's explore the meaning of these philosophies. Hedonism is the pursuit of sensual pleasure. The world is driven by pleasure, viewed by many as the highest good. Hedonistic people seek immediate gratification. The term "sex sells" is what drives Hollywood and the music industry. Many live by the philosophy *if it feels good to you, do it*; sex is held at the highest regard. The philosophy of *materialism* denies the existence of the spirit world and believes and lives only by that which is physical. Materialism refers to the doctrine that material success, possessions, and progress are the highest values in life.$_1$ American culture pushes materialism, valuing the possession of material things and physical comfort above that of spiritual needs. The underpinning of materialism is greed and covetousness. Having traveled abroad, I see the influence of western culture in other countries where the pursuit of material wealth and pleasure is regarded as good and acceptable above spirituality.

Egoism and Individualism

Egoism exalts self-interest as the foundation from which life is lived—personal interest becomes the motive for every choice a person makes, whether that involves relationships, careers, and, unfortunately, morality. *Egoism* is pure self-centeredness. *Individualism* is the principle of being self-reliant and independent. The personality characteristic of individualistic people is one in which they insist on charting their own path and being in control of everything. Individualistic people crave independence. They have no place for God or the Christian values that call us to a life of total dependence on God. Individualism is really just egoism in disguise. The Bible states in 1 John:

> For all that is in the world, the lust of the flesh (craving for sensual gratification) and the lust of the eyes (greedy longings of the mind) and the pride of life, (assurance in one's own resources or in the stability of earthly things) these do not come from the Father but are from the world (itself). (2:16 AMP)

Having ambition to possess and be something more than that which you have and are created to be is coveting. John expressed that longing for erotic pleasure outside of marriage, material things, and self-reliance are of this world and are not of the kingdom of heaven. He urges us not to covet and not love the world or the things in it. This world and the righteous are on a collision course but righteousness will win the day. Nonetheless, a godless society is notorious for coveting what someone else has and what one does not need.

Bombarded with the World

We are living in a culture of instant access. Since the advent of computers and smartphones, our access to information has improved greatly. We have witnessed a rapid progression in technology where we now live in what's known to be a digital age, or what some may like to call the new media age. Social media has changed the way we communicate and how we engage the marketplace. As a result of the inflow of information, we are constantly bombarded with images, subliminal messaging, multicultural influences, political sway, and vain philosophies of the world that are at odds with our spiritual make-up. (We will discuss some of this in chapter 7.)

We are inundated with philosophies of coveting and lust. They are promoted through the airways of nearly every media outlet. Hollywood's influence reaches mainstream America and the rest of the world in droves. What was once taboo has become commonplace. Wrong is right, right is wrong. (Isaiah 5:20) Viewing nakedness, sex, and sexual acts has become the norm—not to mention the intensified affinity towards watching violent shows, shows filled with terror, and witchcraft. I know it's debatable, but these are outlets the enemy uses to promulgate mass murders as he preys on the mentally unstable and those who are demonized.

The crafty art of desensitization is successfully making people indifferent and unresponsive to the world's way of life. Sin flashes across the screen and no one flinches. Sin is welcomed and applauded. Many have inadvertently relied on the social structure of reality to define what is important, meaningful, and true in life. Beauty, wealth, and fame have become the drug of the day with the advent of reality TV. We are bombarded with images and messages that aim at influencing our opinions, our attitudes, our desires, and our behaviors. Propaganda is at work under the guise of subliminal messaging that constructs the ideologies of our social, political, and spiritual spheres. Satan uses the tool of propaganda as roadblocks to dumb down society. Satan also uses media outlets as a means to control and to keep people blind and in darkness. He is very calculating and intentional in his pursuit to keep you in bondage.

We have discussed Satan in detail in the previous chapter, but it is important to know how he interjects himself in the world to create roadblocks that will keep you preoccupied with the happenings in the world instead of your destiny. Satan knows your worth and your value. Think about that…if you did not have great worth and value, Satan would not waste time working behind the scenes to create stumbling blocks he erects through the world. He knows that in the day that you come to recognize your true identity, you will not only come to understand the schemes of the wicked one, but you will also be empowered through the knowledge of your self-worth and your value that's derived in God. That empowerment will allow you to put an end to every plan and trap plotted by the enemy in this world for your life.

False Affiliations

As previously stated, the way we communicate has changed dramatically over the last two decades. People once valued face-to-face encounters, letter writing, and phone calls. Now, people text on their smartphones and chat via social media. The advent of social media isn't a bad thing in and of itself, but the problem lies in the deception of it all. It is designed to bring people closer together, but in actuality, it has caused people to become more isolated and dejected. Many viewers of social media compare themselves to others. We are often not mindful of the reality that what we see on social media is only a highlight reel of the best parts of people's lives.

The lie that someone else's life is better than your own is a roadblock that is wreaking havoc in the lives of many. No one ever posts pictures of abuse or addiction. No one posts pictures of their marriage on the verge of divorce, or pictures of boyfriends cheating. Have you ever seen pictures of one having to relocate because they lost a job, or pictures at a doctor's office revealing patients who have some terminal disease? People wouldn't fathom posting pictures of how they are in need of meds because they have become clinically depressed, and so on. Social media was designed to make people happy, connected, productive, and satisfied, yet it has done the complete opposite. A lot of people are unhappy, disconnected, unproductive, and frustrated in life due to the roadblock of social media. I can continue this rant, but I think you get the gist. The point I am making here is that things are not as they seem. This world's system is alluring and deceptive. The sooner you are aware of its gravitational pull on your life, the better you will be able to navigate around the roadblocks it places before you on your way to discovering your identity.

CHAPTER SEVEN

The Flesh: The Battle Within

7
The Flesh: The Battle Within

Much like the roadblocks erected in the world, your flesh poses a major obstruction to the discovery of your identity. The term "flesh" can take on several meanings as it can be defined in different ways. However, I will attempt to provide you with a tangible understanding of what it means so you can identify the battle within. When referring to the flesh within our specific context, we are not referring to your body, but rather *to your nature*. Once we are born again, we are a new creation unto God (2 Corinthians 5:17), and our newness comes with a new nature. The flesh is then your old self, that part of you before Christ, without God. The idea of without God is something I want to focus on here.

Without God

The moment we enter the world, we inherently function in our flesh, in our old sin nature. No one has to tell a child how to have a tantrum; they do it automatically. My son, when he was four years old, threw a toy on top of the roof. When I asked him, "Did you throw that on the roof?", he replied, "No! The little rascals did it." Albeit funny, you see, no one has to teach a child how to lie and place blame on others; it is innate—it is the sin nature. According to the Word of God, we were by "nature the children of wrath." (Ephesians 2:3) What this means is that we are *physically born alive in sin and spiritually dead unto God*. From birth we didn't have means to communicate with God or have relationship with him; neither was the knowledge of Him retained in any member of our being. So we lived in our flesh, in our sin nature, which alienates us from God and cause us to act independently from God.

Internal Conflict

In Christ, we are made alive spiritually. And through Him, we live as new spiritual beings in an earthly body. The old nature or old man did not die at our conversion. The flesh remains very much alive and at work, while the spirit is very much alive and at work. We began to experience conflict within our soul because the two entities are at odds. This conflict is the flesh warring against the spirit. As stated by Paul,

> For the desires of the flesh are opposed to the [Holy] Spirit, and the [desires of the] Spirit are opposed to the flesh(Godless human nature) for these are antagonistic to each other [continually withstanding and in conflict with each other], so that you are not free but are prevented from doing what you desire to do."(Galatians 5:17 AMP)

You are now a spirit being and your true identity is tied to that. The flesh is an entity that is hostile to God and it will continuously impede the pursuit of your identity. "The flesh is self-reliant rather than God-dependent; it is self-centered rather than Christ centered."[1] The perfect picture of how we are to live as Christians in this flesh is seen in the very life of Jesus. In John's account of the Father's witness to the Son, he quotes Jesus as follows:

> "I am able to do nothing from Myself **(independently, of My own accord, but only as I am taught by God and as I get His orders)**. Even as I hear, I judge **(I decide as I am bidden to decide. As the voice comes to Me, so I give a decision)**, and My judgment is right **(just, righteous)**, because I do not seek or consult My own will **(I have no desire to do what is pleasing to Myself, My own aim, My own purpose)** but only the will and pleasure of the Father Who sent Me." (John 5:30 AMP)

Even Jesus had to discern the thoughts that went through His mind. He distinguished between the voices of Satan, society, and His own voice in order to hear the voice of God. Any thoughts that were not from the Father or contrary to the Father's heart, Jesus condemned in order that His judgments would be just and righteous. He lived a life totally dependent on the Father and not His flesh. Jesus always consulted the Father's will for His life. His desires were that of pleasing the Father.

While our flesh desires what pleases it, Jesus desired what pleased the Father. The world categorizes dependence as weakness while admiring the man or woman who can be free to please himself or herself unabated before others. But true strength is in the one who can allow the God who created him full control, and true virtue is found in the one who has power to restrain his self-seeking fleshly desires and place Jesus Christ and others before himself. The propensity to live independent of God will become a major roadblock on your path to discovering your identity. In a world that highly regards independence and self-autonomy, Jesus demonstrated dependence on God. It was through His dependence on Father God that he was able to arrive at autonomy. The same is applicable for us. Our reliance on God will remove any and all obstructions that prevent the realization of our identity.

Works of Flesh vs. Works of Spirit

The flesh and the Spirit are two existing forces that lie within and they are constantly warring with one another. The book of Galatians outlines the dichotomy of these two opposing forces. The works of the flesh are these: adultery, fornication, uncleanness, lasciviousness(being filled with or showing sexual desire), idolatry, witchcraft, hatred, variance (not in harmony, disagreement), emulations (efforts to match/compete or exceed another person often by means of replication and copying that person), wrath (extreme anger), strife (conflict, anger and bitterness over irrelevant issues), seditions (to incite others to disobey laws and or their government), heresies (an opinion or practice that is divergent and conflicting with the truth), envying (wanting what someone else has), murder, drunkenness, reveling (drinking excessively), and many more works of the flesh. (Galatians 5:19-21) The works of the Spirit are completely opposite to the works of the flesh. According to the New Living Translation, the Holy Spirit produces fruit that is "love, joy, peace, patience, kindness, goodness, faithfulness, gentleness, and self-control." (Galatians 5:22-23 NLT) The contradiction between the two works clearly highlights the dichotomy of right vs. wrong, good vs. evil, and selfishness vs. selflessness.

The two opposing positions are contrary to one another. The Spirit will always be in opposition to the flesh, and daily we must choose either to walk in the works of the flesh or the works of the Spirit. This battle between the Spirit and the flesh is often the main roadblock on our way to discovering our true identity. The answer to our true selves cannot be found absent of a relationship and understanding of God. In our pursuit of God we must inquire of Him for clarity of identity. Who better to consult about our identity than the One who created man to begin with?

It is the works of the flesh that cause our relationship with God to become clouded and estranged, our hearing dull, and our hearts hardened toward the only One who can provide us clarity of identity. The works of the flesh ultimately promote self and all self-interests. They create a barrier in our lives that obstruct the fruitful work of the Spirit. Our good works should be a by-product of God's Spirit living within us. The battle within is relentless, but must be won if we desire to gain wisdom to unearth our true identity.

SECTION THREE

The Seat of All Affection:
Your Soul

CHAPTER EIGHT

Self-Imprisonment

8
Self-Imprisonment

I was recently reviewing the incarceration rate and found some staggering statistics. There are approximately 2 million people incarcerated here in the U.S. The NAACP estimation is 2.3million, to be exact. With America being only 5% of the world's population, it incarcerates about 25% of the world's prisoners, according to data pulled from the years1980–2008.[1] I'm sure these figures have increased since that study. These statistics simply reflect those that are noted on record. But did you know that an even more alarming fact exists? It is that millions upon millions of people, both in the U.S. and abroad, are being imprisoned daily by the strongholds that exist in the mind, will, and emotions. This self-imprisonment has robbed most all of humanity from the life God intended for us to live.

The Mind

This chapter will discuss how the mind works. It is a bit technical but important for understanding the part of the soul that houses thoughts. Your life is controlled by your thoughts. How meaningful and complete your life is will be determined by the thoughts you think. In order to discover your true self you must be aware of your thoughts and the power of the mind. I define the "self" as the soulish part of man. The soul is made up of three parts: the mind, will, and emotions. The soul is the seat of our affections and is also the place where strongholds exist. These strongholds fuel the problems you encounter in life and they originate in the realm of the soul. There is always a cause-and-effect to every event in life. The cause is an initial premise or catalyst that precipitates a result, effect, or condition. As we focus on the mind's involvement on the issues of life, we will uncover some truths that will alter soulish identity and prayerfully lead you to freedom.

Understand this: Our lives are a direct reflection of how we think. How you think of yourself determines the paths you will

Self-Imprisonment

take in life. Oftentimes, it is our thoughts that initiate an outcome. In dealing with the crisis of the identity, we must be aware of how the crisis starts in the mind. Our thoughts are powerful, and I hope to demonstrate that as we go along.

Example of the Soul at Work

I will never forget this diagram I had to learn in graduate school. This isn't an exact replica but it looked something like this—and we will view this model several different ways to get to the essence of its meaning.

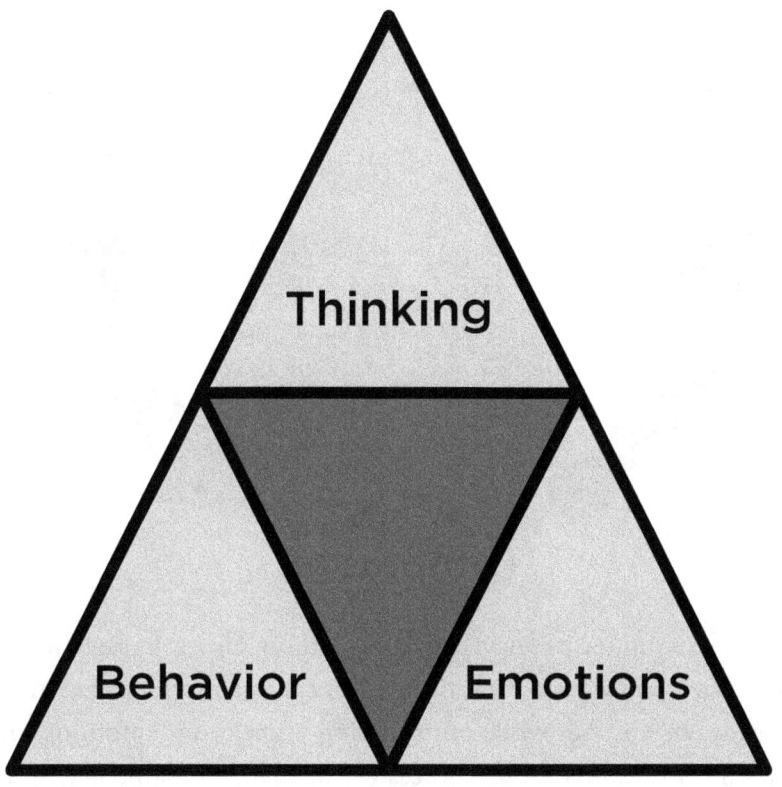

The key concept here is that our thinking impacts our emotions, and our emotions affect our behavior (actions of the will or choices made). The same can be said in reverse: Our behavior impacts our emotions, our emotions impact our thinking. This process has within it continuity between thoughts, feelings, and actions. Your thoughts and feelings serve as your cause and your actions serve as the effect—the outcome of your thinking and feeling. This notion becomes more concrete when we apply the concept that our emotions and behavior are both an internal and external display of what we are thinking and what we believe. I often conceptualized the visual aid in the previous diagram in a different manner as follows.

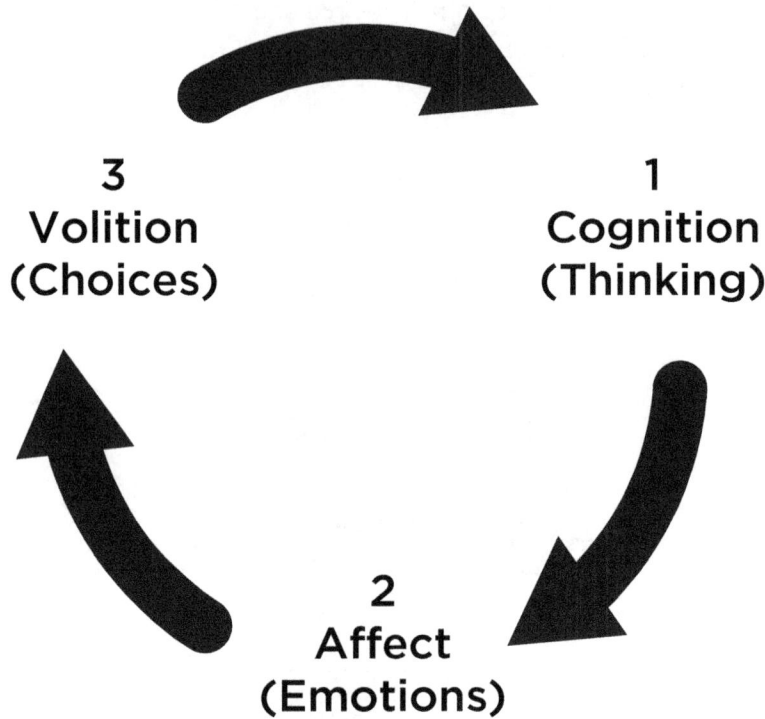

As you can see, we have the same components at work here, but this allows you to understand this concept in a more fluid manner. The idea here is that while our thinking impacts our emotions, and our emotions impact our choices (behaviors), the same is emphasized in reverse. In the graphic above, the three parts of the soul are easily seen as forces that are always at work. For every action, there is a reaction. This process is cyclical, ever-flowing from one element of the soul to another, constantly influencing one another at times when we are both conscious and unconscious of the processes at work.

I numbered the three components of the soul so we can look at an example of how this progression takes place. This cyclical process first triggers thoughts, which influence feelings, which determine the choices we make on any given day. First, our cognitive process is voluntarily or involuntarily at work by the ingesting of thoughts. Once you think on something long enough, your affect, or emotions, are triggered. Your emotions and feelings concerning a matter are involuntarily at work, meaning, your emotions naturally and automatically surface without effort. Finally, you voluntarily act out of the emotions that arise and are felt. Your actions are your volitions or the choices you make, based on your thinking and emotions. The choices you make are your behavioral chain reaction—they are your actions based on your reactions to the thoughts and feelings concerning any given matter.

What Comes First?

I was having a similar discussion about this process with a dear friend in Trinidad about the power of mind and how that internal process impacts other components of the soul. Our continuity of thought, emotions, and choices are indicators and predictors of our life's outcome. For example, if you are experiencing happiness and success, then you are likely to have a healthy balance at work in your soul. (However, this is not always the case, as some people use their accolades and success to hide their insecurity and inadequacies that exist in other areas of life.)

If you are experiencing physical and emotional defeat, then it is very likely that there is an unhealthy imbalance at work within your soul. My friend asked me, "What comes first, the chicken or the egg?" In essence, her point was that the process within the soul that typically starts with a thought, can—on other occasions—start with the emotions, speech, or actions—and these can also trigger good or bad thoughts. For example, it becomes a cyclical process of speaking, feeling, and behavior (actions and choices) that cultivates thought and perpetuates negative or positive thinking. These progressions become the underpinning from which our life's outcome is determined.

Here is the thing: The process of cause and effect can be reversed within the soul. I'm sure you have had moments where you did something and then regretted it. Your actions and the feelings associated with your choice sparked an onslaught of thoughts about what you think and how you feel about yourself. This is the reversal process at work. However, I will assert that before your emotions and your volitions start to initiate a reaction, they have first started in the mind (thought life) at some point. This is where we have to hone in on the ideal of *conscious vs. unconscious thought*.

Conscious vs. Unconscious Thought

We are aware of conscious thought, but not the unconscious thought (involuntary thinking). The *unconscious thought* is the thought process that has been constructed by the world around us from the time we are born, up through the early childhood stages in life. At some point in the early stages of life, this way of thinking is sealed off and thoughts come up from the unconscious all throughout life. Conscious thought comes out of the conscious mind—the thinking mind, the educated, and the intellectual mind. The unconscious mind is the emotional mind.$_2$ Your conscious mind can accept or reject information that comes into it but the unconscious or subconscious cannot. That emotional part of the unconscious mind gets involved with the thoughts in the conscious mind and it will dictate what happens in your life. I have stated previously that we have to be intentional about thinking; challenging our thoughts in order to determine that we live life thinking in a manner that aligns with our true self which is found in Christ.

The manner in which you wake up each morning and start your day derives from unconscious thought. You do not have to intentionally think, *Okay, I'm up now, I need to use the bathroom, I need to wash my face, now I need to brush my teeth, next I should eat breakfast, iron my clothes, I have to shower, and now I can go to work* . . . No, you just do it. And how you start your day is right to you, because you learned it in early childhood. Conversely, your routine of getting up and out in the morning can seem ineffective to another, and they may start their day entirely different based on unconscious thought patterns learned during childhood. We can look at this as learned behavior, *but I want you to see that it all comes from a process of automatic thinking originating in unconscious thought.* We are influenced and operate out of unconscious thought all the time. Our unconscious thought defines for us daily what is right or wrong, what is socially acceptable, who we are, and what we can do. These theoretical constructs are learned from parental figures, family, friends, and people in authority, as well as the influence of television and movies, the web, and other things.

Importance of the Mind

Your mind-thought process is important to your health and stability in life. It is the seat of all your affection. Out of it flows life, and you determine the sort of life that comes from it. I'm sure that as you are reading this, you can start to identify thoughts you have been thinking about yourself and others that stem from childhood. If anything in your thought life warrants change, in order for you to truly ascertain your true identity, you will have to be proactive and consciously work to alter those thoughts to line up with the Word of God. The key to discovering your true identity (true self) must start in the mind; you have to change your thinking! Joseph Prince puts it this way, *"Right believing produces right living."*₃ Your *right thinking* and your *right believing* will produce for you healthy emotions, and your healthy emotions will produce sound choices. Begin to think differently and every other part of the soul will align to flow in harmony with your mind. You have to be deliberate in your thinking. Your thoughts are the seeds to the fruit your life will produce.

CHAPTER NINE

The Emotions

9
The Emotions

Your emotions were created and given to you by God. Emotions can be good or bad. Having negative emotions aren't always bad, but having negative emotions too often is unproductive. Unconstructive emotions are roadblocks to understanding your identity. Having stability in your emotions is important as they are manifestations of your thoughts. Your emotions were never designed to be the part of you that rule over you. The thing about emotions is that they are fickle. You can be up today and down tomorrow, inspired one minute and uninspired the next, encouraged then discouraged all in one day—shall I say more? If left unchecked, your emotions will lead you off course and right out of the will of God for your life. You will never know your true identity if you are driven by the dictates of your emotions.

Your emotions also lack discipline; they want what they want when they want it, and if they are getting what they want, they demand more of it. Your emotions will tell you, *I'm tired, I don't care,* or *I'm going to give them a piece of my mind.* They may say *stay angry, be sad,* or even tell you one morning *I don't feel like going to work,* and so on. Obey your emotions long enough and you will find yourself out of a job—not to mention unhappy with life in general! There are many other examples I can make about the dictates of emotions, like: Spend money you don't have, continue to use drugs, stay in that relationship you know God is calling you out of, continue drinking in excess and using drugs, continue watching porn . . . the emotional dictates of the flesh are endless. These examples may seem trivial, but don't miss the point: Listen to the carnality of your emotions and find yourself stressed, depressed, broke, waddling in ruin and decay. You get the point.

Control Your Emotions or They Will Control You

You must control your emotions or they will control you. I can declare to you that every person who lacks discipline, self-control, and temperance in the area of their emotions is unstable in life and have never come to know their true identity. Your life cannot be lived in accordance with whichever way the pendulum of emotions swings. Your flesh will always be in opposition to the will and plan of God for your life.

Sadly, I have witnessed people who cannot control their emotions make serious mistakes that they later deeply regret. I was one of those people. Such mistakes have led people to living unstable, tormented, anxiety-driven lives. Be led by your emotions and you will drive people away. When emotions rule, people often become destitute as a result of not being able to stay faithful, or become angry, bitter, critical, resentful, undisciplined, and wasteful all the time. Your emotions will cause you to want much but do less.

Example of Anxiety

The Bible has much to say on mastering our emotions. Let's look at a few scriptures that shed light on the topic. On the topic of worry and anxiety, the book of Philippians says, "Do not be anxious about anything, but in everything by prayer and supplication with thanksgiving let your requests be made known to God. And the peace of God, which surpasses all understanding, will guard your hearts and your minds in Christ Jesus." (4:6-7) I can guarantee you that worrying and carrying around anxiety over a matter has never brought any resolution to the problem.

Example of Anger

We've all been around an angry person. It's like walking on eggshells; you never know what will set them off! Angry people either cause the people around them to live in fear and resent them, or they push people out of their lives. "A hot-tempered man stirs up strife, but he who is slow to anger quiets contention." (Proverbs 15:18) Angry people are people who lack control over their emotions and they ride the tempest of anger every time it rears its ugly head. On the other hand, the man or woman who has self-control will not be led by their emotions and has power to live a quiet and peaceable life.

According to Proverbs, "A glad heart makes a cheerful face, but by sorrow of heart the spirit is crushed." (15:13) Distress, disappointment, misfortune, low self-esteem, low self-worth and the like are often well-kept secrets that eat away at you. Before you know it, your spirit is crushed and a crushed spirit sees no hope and no reason to be optimistic. What a miserable, lonely way to go through life. Yet, many do—they suffer in silence while *masking* the source of their pain. This robs them of truly living life.

Emotions Are Deceptive and Ambiguous

Here's the thing about your emotions: They are deceptive and ambiguous. Being controlled by desires will keep you in a constant state of flux. Paul writes to the Galatians urging them to "walk by the Spirit, and you will not gratify the desires of the flesh. For the flesh desires what is contrary to the Spirit, and the Spirit what is contrary to the flesh. They are in conflict with each other, so **that you are not to do whatever you want.**" (Galatians 5:16-17 NIV)

Paul goes on to say that the working of the flesh, or emotions, is apparent when you act out in sexual immorality, impurity, sensuality, idolatry, sorcery, enmity, strife, jealousy, fits of anger, rivalries, dissensions, or divisions. (Galatians 5:19-21) The things you wish to do and accomplish in life will never become visible until you gain discipline in the area of your emotions. You may achieve some level of success in life but a lack of discipline in the area of emotions will not be able to keep you there nor bring fulfillment while you are there. None of the works of the flesh that Paul mentioned above will bring you emotional wholeness; and they certainly will not lead you to the discovery of your true identity.

Teachable Moment from a Dream

I had a dream one year at a time when I was struggling with my emotions, and not to mention, the enemy was really trying to trap me with temptation. I know you have probably been in a situation where if God did not intervene, you could not trust yourself to do the right thing. This is where I was. I was afraid of turning back to my former ways because I was growing tired of dealing with the present circumstances. So one night, God spoke to me in a dream like he typically does when I don't take the time to consult Him intentionally about my issues. God uses the time he can get my attention—when I am sleeping.

In the dream, I was driving a car with my son, Joshua, in the backseat and there was this guy in the front seat who was contrary to the will of God for my life, and yes, temptation was present. As I tried driving my car down this long, curvy, winding road, at every turn I almost had an accident. I was driving knowing I was so out of control that I was about to have a terrible accident. All the while, Mr. Temptation was sitting in the passenger seat like nothing unusual was happening. I came to a pit stop in the road and decided I must stop the car and tell Mr. Temptation to get out. After I did this, I put my son, Joshua, in the front seat and took off—leaving Mr. Temptation in my rearview mirror, never to look back. And what do you know, my car stopped swerving! I regained control of the vehicle and drove safely the rest of the way.

Dream Interpretation

Well, I was sure of what God was trying to tell me: Mr. Temptation was appealing greatly to my emotions, my flesh. And if the flesh had its way, I would have taken Mr. Temptation and driven off into the sunset. But the thing about sin is that it satisfies for only a little while and then you are left with feelings of regret, shame, and guilt. Sin robs you spiritually, emotionally, physically, and relationally. It is never worth it! If I had continued with Mr. Temptation and given in to the appetites of my flesh, I would have spent my real life out of control, out of the will of God. You can bet your bottom dollar that destruction would be sure to follow in other ways. The problem with sin is that it never just affects you. It is like a cancer that spreads into every aspect of your life adversely affecting you *and* the people around you.

Coming to a pit stop allowed me to make a choice. I had to either choose my way, what I wanted, what would satisfy my flesh for a moment, or choose the one who could give me true and lasting satisfaction. I had to choose the one who could put my life back on the right path to peace, safety, harmony with God, and sweet fellowship with the people around me. You see my son, Joshua, was an important symbol in the dream. My son didn't have the power to keep me from sin, but his name did.

The name "Joshua" is found in the Old Testament. As you may know, the Old Testament original manuscripts were written in Hebrew, the Israelites' language. The name "Joshua" in the Hebrew translates to *Yahushua* (depending on different spellings, it is *Yehoshua* or *Jehoshua*)$_1$ and the Yahushua transliteration in the Greek is *Iesous*$_2$ which is "Jesus" translated in the English. Yahushua is Joshua, meaning, "the Lord is Salvation." This is why the symbolism of my son in the dream is significant. He was a representation of Jesus Christ. There is great power in the name of Jesus! Jesus saves and delivers us as often as we need him, for as long as we choose him. *Jesus is the only one who is able to keep our life on course.* When we refuse to be led by our emotions and the desires of the flesh, we are actually saying, *I want more out of life!* When we can stand up to our feelings and say, *NOT TODAY!* we exercise self-control and the discipline needed to uncap our identity.

Final Word

If you give in to your flesh (your emotions) in life, you will reap from those emotions some of the following: regret, setback, heartache, disappointment, pain, loneliness, guilt, shame, and more. See, emotions are always fluctuating and if you are ruled by them, your life will never be stable. However, when you yield yourself to the Spirit of God and choose to live life God's way, you will reap of the life of Christ and all the good that God has to offer you through Christ. Your life will not only be stable, but you will live peaceful, quiet, calm, and contented lives, and in the will of God . . . the ultimate sweet spot! Don't give into your feelings. They are fleeting; don't be led by your emotions they are misleading; don't give into your flesh, it will devour you and draw you away from any chance of experiencing the joy of discovering your true identity.

CHAPTER TEN

The Will

10
The Will

I touched briefly in chapter 8 on the function of the will as it relates to the soul of man. Let's now take an in-depth look at the work of the will. The will of man is the part of us that houses the free will to choose. It is the part of the mind that has the ability to act on the desires of the mind. A deliberate action that comes out of the will is called your volition. Your volitions are simply your decisions, choices, desires, and your preferences. The will chooses our actions and shapes our behaviors. Our actions are outward indications of the thoughts we think and the feelings we feel. Volitions are the by-product of the thought processes of the conscious mind and the subconscious mind—the emotions. For every action (thought-feeling), there is a reaction (your volition). The will is the reaction to your thoughts and your emotions.

When the mind and the emotional components of the soul are out of balance, your actions and behaviors will be, too. Solomon wrote in Proverbs, "There is a way which seems right to a man and appears straight before him, but at the end of it the way of death." (14:12) Imbalance in the soul will always create an illusion as to what is right or what is good. When we make choices out of ignorance, we will habitually make choices that lead to regret, defeat, death, and decay.

Our Ability to Choose Stolen

When I was a child, I often heard the saying, "The devil made me do it." Now, in a broad stroke of the brush, this statement had some validity for those who are without Christ. The ability to choose is a bit distorted when choices are made outside of truth which is Jesus Christ. When we go back to Adam and Eve before the fall, we see where they were created by God, in the image of God. God then gave Adam and Eve dominion (power and authority) over the earth and told them to subdue it. (Genesis 1:26-28) God gave man a legal title deed to the earth. By right it was man, not God, who would inhabit and control the earth. God gave man free will; a choice to live for Him and have a relationship with Him.

God put in the midst of the Garden of Eden the tree of life and the tree of knowledge of good and evil. He made it clear that the day Adam and Eve ate of this tree, they would surely die. This was not a threat; it was the law, God's law. God placed that choice there because in order for there to be real love, one must choose to love. It goes without saying that God loved man, His creation, but would man choose to love Him in return? God desires relationship with us and that relationship has to be mutually desired; it has to be chosen, it cannot be forced. Satan came and tempted Adam and Eve, causing the fall of man. It was then that Satan stole the title deed to earth and all rights, power, and authority humanity had on the earth. Humanity became dead spiritually and would eventually experience physical death, but not before experiencing decay and ruin over time. God in His righteousness and holiness cannot have fellowship with sin. So without Jesus, humanity is dead spiritually—void of the right to choose to have a loving relationship with God and live eternally with Him.

Jesus Redeemed Our Ability to Choose

Here is what Jesus did for you and me: Jesus redeemed the right for man to choose again. We can choose sin which leads to death, or we can choose a relationship with God the Father—which results in eternal life and peace with Him. For years, I heard that when Jesus died on the cross for our sins He was redeeming us back from Satan. This is not true. The truth is, Satan was hoodwinked by the Creator of heaven and earth. We give Satan too much credit; he is not that smart!

Satan was so eager to get rid of Jesus that he used men to crucify Jesus on the cross. At the cross it appeared that Jesus lost, humanity would be spiritually displaced forever, and that Satan won. Satan thought he had ruined Jesus like he did Adam. For one to die spiritually he must live in eternal separation from God because of sin. On the cross Jesus died spiritually; it was evident when he cried out, "My God, my God, why have you forsaken me?"(Matthews 27:46) In that moment, Jesus was cut off—separated from the Father—because the sins of humanity were placed on Him by the Father. Yet, on the third day, God the Father would raise Jesus from the dead in a triumphant display of victory over death, hell, and the grave. In this way, Jesus disarmed the rulers of darkness and took back all power and authority usurped by Satan. He shamed them publicly by His victory over them on the cross. (Colossians 2:15 NLT)

Jesus satisfied the demand of God the Father which was that all who sin are worthy of judgment, death, and eternal separation from Him. Jesus redeemed us from God's judgment—the debt accumulated against humanity for its sin. This debt was never what God wanted to hold against humanity, but it was by law what had to be, because sin cannot dwell in the presence of a holy God. The punishment for our sins and for our peace was put on Jesus at the cross.

According to the prophecy of Isaiah, "The LORD [God the Father] was pleased to crush Him [His Son Jesus at the cross], putting Him to grief; if He would render Himself as a guilt offering, He will see His offspring." (53:10 NASB) Jesus became sin; He became guilty before God the Father on behalf of humanity. He became what we are, apart from Him—sin—so that we might become righteous (Him) as He is before God. Now, we can have peace with God, relationship with the God of the universe, and the gift of eternal life through belief in Jesus Christ. Jesus acquitted us legally so we would be found not guilty before the Great Judge, God the Father. Jesus did not redeem us from Satan but rather satisfied the wrath and judgment of God the Father. This is what Jesus did at the cross, and to anyone who believes on Him for He has redeemed your free will to choose. You are no longer a slave to sin and death! You have the power and authority to choose God and love over sin and death.

Teachable Moment from a Dream

My teachable moment cannot top the wonderful truth of what Jesus accomplished for us at the cross, but I hope to illustrate in a practical way that we have free will to choose, and what it can do for you when you choose Christ, righteousness, and love over the flesh. I had a dream recently of being at a variety store that sold a little of everything. I was there shopping with my husband. I watched him from afar as he was shopping in the back of the store and I saw him pick up a bottle of mango alcohol. (Now, note that in real life, my favorite fruit is mango, so it was befitting of the Lord to use this fruit in my dream.) The bottle of mango alcohol looked milky and thick, just like mango juice. If you've ever had mango juice, then you know just what I'm talking about!

As I watched my husband pick up this big bottle, I immediately began to desire it. I could imagine how tasty it would be. I have never had mango alcohol, as this was the case in the dream as well. In any event, I wanted some. So, I went to the back of the store and grabbed a bottle. When I got the bottle, my mind began to race back and forth. *Should I buy this bottle of mango alcohol?* I began to make my way to the check-out counter and on my way, I saw mango fruit on the edge of another counter. I stopped and picked up the fruit. Now, I was comparing the two. I finalized my decision from a financial perspective. I thought it was wiser to buy the mango fruit; it was cheaper and besides, I love mango! When I got to the counter, the cashier began to weigh each mango to determine how much each would cost per pound. When she rang my total, she said, "Congratulations, you got a reward of a dollar! You can use it towards your purchase the next time you come back." Well, I was so excited. I was looking forward to enjoying my mango, but even more so, I was thrilled to get a reward that I wasn't even expecting.

Dream Interpretation

In life, there are ways that seem right to us. Often, our actions mirror the actions and choices of others. Meanwhile, what is right and good for someone else may not be right or good for you. In the dream, I saw my husband pickup the mango alcohol and I wanted it. I could taste it in my mind and it was good! When I saw the bright, fresh fruit, I weighed the benefits of purchasing the mango alcohol vs. the fruit. The fruit was sitting on the edge of a counter. We have to choose wisely in life. Some choices may appear to be on edge—risky because it goes against our mind, will, and emotions.

In choosing the thing that was right and good for me, I was rewarded for my decision. Let's view this in a practical sense: the mango alcohol would have given me immediate gratification. I could have gotten enjoyment out of drinking it. And, if it had tasted anything like mango juice, then I would have gotten in trouble for drinking the entire bottle! While the alcohol would have provided a measure of enjoyment, it would have left me dehydrated and drunk. Eating the mango fruit, on the other hand, was beneficial to my health, my body, and my conscience. I would have no regrets eating the fruit, while at the same time getting many nutritional benefits as mangos are high in vitamin C, A, K, B-6, folate, and potassium—just to name a few.

The point I am making is that we all have to make choices in life. When making these choices, we can't afford to be influenced by our surroundings—by other people, or the world; nor can we be led by our flesh. As you read this, you may be thinking, *What could be wrong with choosing to purchase the mango alcohol?* Consider this: Paul said when he wrote to the church at Corinth, "'I have the right to do anything,' you say, but, not everything is beneficial. 'I have the right to do anything,' but not everything is constructive." (1 Corinthians 10:23 NIV) Another Bible version tells us that not everything is edifying (1 Corinthians 10:23 NASB) —meaning, everything is not good for the nurturing of our spirit or for providing moral or intellectual instructions. Whether we realize it or not, we make choices based on how they benefit us, but some choices give the illusion of reward when they actually bring about punishment! All choices have consequences—good or bad. If you align your volitions with the Word of God, you will find He will be your exceedingly great reward!

Final Word

The outcome of your choices should be nurturing, enlightening, and enriching for your life and the lives of others. Show me someone who makes choices in life within these parameters, and I will show you someone who is wise and disciplined. More so, I will show you someone who has uncapped the characterization of true identity. How you identify yourself will determine the path you take and the decisions you make. Once your choices are intertwined with good judgment, then you can be sure rewards will follow. Whether they are rewards of love, peace, wisdom, health, wealth, or favor in the sight of God and man, they will chase you down. Your volitions are the part of the soul that acts and responds to your thoughts and emotions. They are outward indicators of what is on the inside. You do not have to be a slave to sin or poor choices. Jesus has redeemed your right to choose!

SECTION FOUR

"The Art of War"

CHAPTER ELEVEN

Understanding the Battle

11
Understanding the Battle

My husband has a friend in China who worked here in the States with him for a brief period. Returning to the States from a trip home, he brought a beautiful bamboo scroll with Chinese writing on it as a souvenir for my husband. I asked my husband what it said; he told me the scroll was called *The Art of War*. I admire this unique piece of art and have even put it on display in our home. One day, I walked by and admired it; however, I realized my appreciation for it was hampered by my inability to read and understand Chinese. Thus, I was not able to neither fully comprehend nor truly appreciate this obscure piece of art.

I did a little research and found that *The Art of War* is an ancient Chinese military treaty that was attributed to a high-ranking military general named Sun Tzu. It is distinguished and celebrated in China so much so that most people are well aware of it and even know the history behind it today. *The Art of War* is a comprehensive work on military strategy, military tactics, and business tactics. Sun Tzu's work was written over 2,500 years ago and has been studied by many military and business elites in the world because of its teaching people on how to avoid disaster.₁ This composition has influenced eastern and western cultures, and has fashioned how many countries organize their military thinking, business strategies, and politics.

Much like this beautiful piece of bamboo scroll with ancient Chinese inscriptions on *The Art of War* that I have in my home, unable to read, understand, or even fully appreciate, I find there to be a similar conundrum with many Christians trying to read their Bibles. When I was growing up—and even today—it is not uncommon to see a Bible on display in a home, yet many fail to study the Word of God. Because of this, they are deficient in wisdom and understanding of the content held in the scriptures.

Understanding the Battle

As Christians it is of vital necessity to become well-studied in *The Art of War*, or should I say the Holy Scriptures. War is always an intentional and premeditated conflict. It is organized and prolonged and is often unavoidable. *We, as Christians, must come to grips with the reality that we are at war whether we want to be or not.* Now that we have that truth out and in the open, we can move onto gaining an understanding of the rules of engagement in warfare.

We have a unique disposition in that we know the end of the story: WE WIN! However, while we are living, we must make every attempt to arm ourselves for all the battles to come. Tzu believed that war was important to a people. He stated, "It is a matter of life and death…it is the way to survival or destruction."₂ Your knowledge of war and how to do battle will determine your survival or destruction. Our adversary is strategic, deliberate, and diligent. Unlike Sun Tzu's philosophy—which holds the belief that war is to be fought swiftly—Satan, on the contrary, believes in patiently studying you all the while he organizes his plans to devour you.

Your adversary intentionally works to deceive, creating roadblocks and mental strongholds that will imprison you. We are not immune to Satan's attacks. You have a fighter within you and He is greater than your adversary. He has also provided you with the tools needed to understand the battle and win the battle through His Word. Know that Satan is always calculating. Your mental, emotional, spiritual, and relational well-being is at jeopardy. Countering his attacks is a matter of life and death, so learn to fight!

Spiritual Warfare

Paul discloses the "art of war" for the Christians in 2 Corinthians. He taught, "The weapons we fight with are not the weapons of the world. On the contrary, they have divine power to demolish strongholds. We demolish arguments and every pretension that sets itself up against the knowledge of God, and we take captive every thought to make it obedient to Christ." (2 Corinthians 10:4-5 NIV) Strongholds are things that bind us. In the context of these scriptures, strongholds are actual headlocks, grips, vises, clinches, and iron grips that Satan sets up in our minds to control us and to keep us confined to every internal argument. These internal arguments are the influences, persuasions, opinions, and urgings that are created by the enemy for you. Satan is so crafty that he places these arguments and imaginations in your mind in the first person. An unskilled warrior would think these false thoughts are actually his own thoughts. Satan also orchestrates a barrage of thoughts and wreaks havoc through mental assaults that are projected into our mind as the *perceived thoughts and opinions of others*. The trap here is thinking that, "If someone else thinks this of me, then it *must* be true!"

False thinking concerning the opinions of others is often one of the cardinal reasons people are tethered to a mental prison! The labels, thoughts, and opinions of others placed on us from childhood and onward become the strongholds that keep us blinded from knowing the truth of who we really are. The real enemy is Satan! Now, does he use people? Yes, he does, but he is at the core of every stronghold there is. He is the one that is behind robbing you of living the life God intends for you to live. Let us remember: "We wrestle not against flesh and blood, but against principalities, against powers, against the rulers of the darkness of this world, against spiritual wickedness in high places." (Ephesians 6:12) Paul tells the believer how to war against the adversary.

We engage in the spiritual "art of war" when we demolish arguments and pretensions, bringing them under the obedience of Christ. We "demolish," meaning, we knock down, tear down, pull down, bulldoze over, blow up, and destroy every thought that rises up against the knowledge of God, or the truth of what God's Word says about us. Any thoughts that are contrary to who God is are arguments. *Arguments* are influences, a point of view, or opinions. *Pretenses* are affections, desires, posturing, self-exultation, or self-centeredness. All-in-all, these are mental blocks designed to keep you from the knowledge of God and, ultimately, the knowledge of your true identity. Paul's instruction on warfare in 2 Corinthians 10:4-5 teaches us how to hold our ground from a defensive perspective, and a good one at that. Let me instruct you from an offensive perspective.

A Teachable Moment from the Lord

One night I was praying and the Lord spoke to me and said "I need you to see me…see my heart…see my name on you." I sat pondering what exactly He meant by saying "see me," "see my name on you." Now, when someone generally says, "I want you to see me," we have a basic connotation as to what that means. There is a basic understanding of seeing someone physically, in a tangible fashion. Although Jesus is alive, I cannot see Him physically unless He decides to reveal Himself in that manner. And let's face it: that does not happen to people often. Then there is the understanding that when asked to see Him, He was saying, *I want you to look a little closer, see past the exterior and peer into my heart.* Was this what the Lord was telling me to do? After thinking intently about this I came to believe He was telling me to see Him as the true Savior that He is, and not how I imagine Him.

So I wondered *who He is truly,* realizing that my understanding of Him only scratches the surface. I could see I was making progress with breaking down the meaning of His invitation to "see me," but I sensed there was more to this request—or should I say instruction—given by the Lord to "see Him," to "see His heart," and to "see His name on me." I figured I needed to continue thinking in order to get a better understanding. After contemplating this directive from the Lord for some time, I do believe He allowed me to arrive at this thought: In order for me to see Him, see His heart, and His name on my life, I had to find a way to see Him how He wanted me to see Him.

Now, I could not physically see Him so I had to see Him spiritually. To be real with you here, I am not always in a spiritual state of mind. Oh, how I wish that were the case, but it's not. So, there was something more to seeing that I needed to understand. Suddenly, I had an *aha!* moment. I had to see Him with my mind. Yes, the Spirit of God began to show me that my mind was the key to seeing Jesus the way He was instructing me to see Him. Then, the question came up within me, *How and why should I see Him with my mind?* Yes, I asked these questions of the Lord. I am very curious and He always satisfies my curiosity.

Light vs. Darkness

The *how* was easy. The way I was going to see Him with my mind was through study and meditation on His Word and time spent in prayer. This answered the how. But the *why* still lingered. Why was it important for me to see Him with my mind? Let's take a moment to consider a parable on light and darkness. Darkness represents ignorance (unawareness) and light represents knowledge and understanding. There is an on-and-off switch in the mind of everyone living. Light is the "on" switch, and darkness the "off" switch. Light and darkness are enemies of one another. Darkness's mission is to seize, conquer, bring diseases and death, and to rule through abusive, oppressive dictatorship.

Those who live in ignorance live in darkness with their "lights turned off." This darkness is the real enemy to those who live in ignorance. Those living in darkness constantly move trying to find freedom, but every time they try to escape, they stumble over something or bump into a wall. While they have hopeful intentions of escaping to freedom, they only suffer injury and brutality. Let's face it. Who can see present danger like walls or a giant pothole in the road in pure darkness? Satan's forces who live in darkness sit back and laugh because all they really have to do is watch, wait, and ruin while people move about in darkness.

Those who live in the light have knowledge and understanding. The light enables them to see. Those who live in light are able to look out and behold the beauty of life; they enjoy the diversity and the awesomeness of God's creation. And, metaphorically speaking, when they come up on giant potholes in the road (stumbling blocks in life), they are able to cross them or travel around them in peace and with ease. They never bump into walls (spiritual roadblocks) because they have light enough to see every wall (obstacle or trial) that exists.

Satan attempts to conquer them; he attempts to stricken them with disease; he even tries hard to rule over them through abuse and oppressive dictatorship, but he can never thrive. The enemy cannot succeed because every time enemies of light attempt to step into the light, their cover of darkness diminishes; they are weakened and are reduced to nothingness. Darkness does not and cannot coexist in light; neither can light coexist in darkness. You cannot conflate the two. You cannot call evil good and good evil because they are polar opposites. (Isaiah 5:20) Please get this in your spirit: God is light and in Him is no darkness at all. (1 John 1:5b)

The mind is the primary source to the flow of life. Knowing God and understanding Him is light. When you can see Jesus with your mind, revelation of your identity becomes clear. What you behold on an on-going basis, you become. See Jesus and be changed…see Jesus and know who you are. Seeing Jesus allows us access to light. In the light you will come to know your purpose in life, and your inheritance in Christ! And this is the driving force that dismantles all manner of darkness, deception, strongholds, and anything else Satan, your adversary, may try to throw your way. *Seeing is believing, and perception is reality.* Intentional thought—with the help of the Holy Spirit of God to understand Jesus Christ—creates the ability to see Him in the mind; seeing reveals who you are. Christ Jesus is your compass in life, the light needed to navigate this world successfully.

How to See

It is important to know that having this capacity to see cannot be achieved in your own doing-effort. When we desire Christ and ask for His aid, He will then facilitate the process of seeing and knowing Him through His Spirit. Jesus said the Holy Spirit "will guide you into all the truth; for He will not speak on His own initiative, but whatever He hears, He will speak; and He will disclose to you what is to come." (John 16:13) We all need the Holy Spirit of God to guide us and assist us in our ability to see Jesus Christ. He is the perfect gentleman. He will not impose Himself on you nor will He take advantage of you, but rather give you the advantage by enabling you to see Jesus Christ through His own lenses.

Now, let's recall the statement the Lord made to me: "I want you to see my name on you." I shared this because everything God teaches us is also meant for others. Jesus said in Matthew, "What I say to you in the dark, tell in the light; and what you hear whispered in the ear, proclaim upon the housetop. (10:27 AMP) I hope I have helped you see how you can see Jesus and change. I am going to share something else in hopes of sealing that understanding. In the next chapter I will provide an illustration that will help you understand the significance in the Lord's desire for not just me but all that read this book to *see Him and His name on you.*

CHAPTER TWELVE

You Have the Advantage

12
You Have the Advantage

Right after graduate school, I moved to Charlotte, North Carolina. I was in the process of looking to buy a house and I needed a certain amount of money for a down payment so my mortgage would be at an affordable rate. While starting a new job and continuing my goal of home ownership, I moved in with my elderly uncle to stay until I was able to save enough money to achieve my dream of home ownership. Then one day, I came home from work to find my uncle sobbing. I asked, "What's the matter?" He went on to tell me that the people who came to look in on him were not going to be able to help him anymore. He feared what would happen to him now that he had no one to take care of him as most of his family was deceased. The few surviving relatives he had lived in other states. He had no one. It hurt to see him this way, so I told him to stop crying, and I assured him that I would care of him. Shortly after becoming his caretaker, I became his financial power of attorney (POA).

Teachable Moment

I want to share with you the process of becoming my uncle's POA, the powers and authority granted, and how that life experience ties to the Lord's instructions to "see my name on you." After my uncle asked me to be his financial POA and I accepted his request, he called his lawyer to draft legal POA papers. The legal documents discussed in detail all the rights—power and authority—I would be granted. My uncle gave me power to manage the entire gamut of his financial responsibilities from bank accounts, investments, real estate, business endeavors—you name it. If it had to do with his finances, he conceded all power and authority to me.

The lawyer gathered the paperwork and a legal witness, which was a notary public. This person was needed to authenticate the identity of the principle (my uncle) and verify the identity of the agent (me) before witnessing his signature on the legal documents.

The notary public's witness and seal stamp on the POA documents reduced the chance that an outside party would contest it. And if it were to be disputed, the courts would rule in my favor because it met all of the state of North Carolina's legal requirements. After the lawyer reviewed all power and authority given to me, my uncle signed the documents. His signature sealed the documents as the document (POA) actually stated "SEAL" beside his signature. The notary public then signed it and stamped the document with her notary public seal. The lawyer then took the documents and filed them with the state of North Carolina with the register of deeds in Mecklenburg County courts. Copies of the documents were mailed to me to keep as proof when dealing with any financial institutions. After officially becoming my uncle's POA, I took the documents to all financial entities my uncle had dealings with and they made copies to be kept on file.

I began to notice that every time I visited a financial institution on my uncle's behalf they would say things like, *Thank you, Miss Wicker. Can I do anything else for you? Can I interest you in any other investment opportunities?* At first, this bothered me a bit because it was clearly communicated that all the business I was doing was on behalf of my uncle and all the money was his, not mine. I got tired of feeling the need to correct them. I was becoming frustrated. One day the Spirit of God helped me realize that they were speaking to me directly because, by right, I had all the legal power and authority to act on my uncle's behalf. When I understood this, I stopped feeling the need to correct everyone.

The financial institutions never saw my uncle, but they were interacting with me as if I was my uncle (as if he was right there), and whatever I said was the final authority and they had to act on that. In essence, my uncle had given me his name, and his name and my name became as one. I did business in his name and all responded just as I would request, because the power of his name that was given to me by law was backed by the financial wealth he had. The amount of his wealth gave me a certain level of clout with all financial institutions. Now for fun, just imagine if you were to become Warren Buffett's POA. The measure of his net worth, $78 billion, would give tremendous influence among financial institutions. The same power and authority he has would be granted to you. You would have the right to use his name in all business endeavors and all entities would have to honor you because of his name, wealth, and influence.

This Is Where You Get the Advantage

The Spirit of the Lord was trying to get me to see His name on me in the very same manner as having my uncle's name placed on my name. The same applies to you. Jesus wants you to see His name on you. When you accepted Jesus as Lord and Savior, you agreed to become His power of attorney. You are now partners with Jesus Christ. I just hope that you will desire to be an active participant in the partnership. For those of you who do want to, this is what Jesus did to give you the advantage.

Jesus gathered a witness—the Father. The Father has authenticated the identity of His Son and verified your identity. The legal paperwork has been drafted, dating back over 2,000 years ago at the cross of Calvary. Jesus read all the rights, authority, and powers He would concede to you. He then signed the documents with His own blood and sealed your POA for handling His business of furthering the ministry of love and reconciliation. The Father sealed the POA documents with His seal of approval because of the righteousness of His Son. The documents have been registered in the courts of heaven and delivered to you through your faith in the Son of the living God. You have copies and proof of your POA in the Word of God. Now, you have all power and authority to carry out the will and plans of Jesus in the earth because you have His name.

He has given you His name. Every child of God has the name of Jesus Christ on his life. Satan and his cohorts cannot contest your spiritual POA. When dealing with Satan, his cohorts, your flesh, and anything of this world, saying the name of Jesus brings Him into direct contact with whatever you are facing. Jesus said that if you ask anything in His name (believing), He would do it. (John 14:14) The power and authority granted to you is backed by the measure of who Jesus is—His righteousness, His health, His wealth, His position, His authority, and His POWER!

God the Father knows what the name of Jesus implies when you say it. He has given you the legal rights to the use of the name that is above every name. The world will respond to you as it did to Him, so long as you see His name on you and use all power and authority given to you in the matchless name of Jesus Christ. His name is your gift. As you come to understand your true identity, your purpose in life—whatever that may be—will become clear to you. God has given you an advantage over the enemy. Satan hates you and he actively makes plans to cause your downfall. But you have greatness on the inside of you. The "art of war" is sealed within your members. You have the warrior of warriors within you who has given you the advantage over your adversary in more ways than one. Let's continue together and I'll show you another way you have the advantage.

Teachable Moment from a Dream

In this dream I was walking with a group of people at night in the dead of winter, and we all knew one another. There were two other people with us who wore the attire of a ninja's uniform. One traveled in front of our group while the other traveled behind. These two men were highly trained warriors who were with us to help and protect us. We went to a carnival and had fun together, but the whole time we were hanging out I sensed that there was trouble ahead of us. I didn't know when it would strike or how the attack would come, but I was certain it would come sooner than we had anticipated. I didn't see a war but somehow knew war was waging.

The two warriors were also very aware of the pending dangers. They were alert and discerning the whole time we were out. After the carnival we headed to one of the group member's home. There we gathered together to have more fun and fellowship. Before playing games we decided to meditate. During this meditation I noticed we all closed our eyes. Some went into a state of complete rest (no-worry zone), some into oblivion, others looked like they could have been sleeping.

Outside, a snowstorm was looming and the wind howling. Something was wrong! During the meditation I had an ominous feeling. I shouted, *something is not right; I can sense something is not right!* I turned to look out the window, only to see two demonic forces appear before my eyes. Dressed as dark knights, they were tall, muscular imps, dressed in black combat uniforms with the most evil gaze I ever saw. They began to make their way towards us to annihilate us.

I yelled out to alert everyone. Fear gripped many hearts as the forces walked towards the house with the attempt to penetrate our walls and obliterate everyone. One of the warriors with us was standing by what looked to be a light switch. He cut it on and light shone down over all of us, fully engulfing the entire room. In that pure white light a mist like tangible dew rested over us. As he turned on the light he said, "Do not be afraid; they cannot see us."

I thanked the Lord and all fear I felt dissipated and we all relaxed and rested in the light. Just as the lights were turned on, the demons were stopped in their tracks. For whatever reason, they were blinded by this light. They became perplexed; completely befuddled. We could hear them converse saying, "Where are they? I thought they were here. Are they in there? We will get them when they come out." As they conversed, they continued to try to peer into the window but could not see us at all.

The warriors who accompanied us were skilled and prepared to fight and aid us in warfare, but not one fought at all...that is physically fought. We were completely safe. We were covered and protected by the glory of God.

After being awakened from this dream I immediately wrote it down and pondered its meaning. I wanted to know what God was trying to tell me so I could convey it to His people.

Interpretation of the Dream

This dream was very significant. The night represents spiritual darkness. The number two can represent witness, union, or division. The two warriors were two witnesses and the two demons were division. The season was winter, which represents an appointed time, a scheduled event, or simply a point in time.[3] All the people hanging out together who were acquainted with one another represent the people of God in union with one another. Then you have the light which represents spiritual purity, truth, and knowledge. The Greek word for light is *phos* (fose) which means, "God is light because light has the extremely delicate, subtle, pure, brilliant quality...the power of understanding."[4]

With the help of the Holy Spirit I came to realize the meaning of the dream. First of all, we are all familiar with cold winter months. In regions where it is cold and snows, the earth is barren. There is little to no life, and we see this as the trees lose their leaves and the grass withers away. Recall in the dream it was a dark winter night and the snow was brewing. God was saying, *In life winter seasons will come and the winds will blow...but will you be ready when they do? There is an appointed time when you will encounter evil, but I have made provision for you.*

Just as the two warriors dressed in what looked to be ninja attire traveled with us—one in the front and the other slightly behind—the Word of God has promised us protection. As stated in Isaiah 58:8 (NIV), "Then your light will break forth like the dawn, and your healing will quickly appear; then your righteousness will go before you, and the glory of the LORD will be your rear guard." In the dream, when we arrived at one of the member's home, we began to meditate. During this meditation I sensed something wrong. It was an actual depiction of how it is impossible for a trial or test to overtake you or come as a surprise when you are meditating on God, His Word, and surrounded by others who are like-minded. Peter instructs us that we should never be caught off guard; "Beloved, think it not strange concerning the fiery trial which is to try you, as though some strange thing happened unto you." (1 Peter 4:12)

The two demons illustrated spiritual alienation and separation from God. Spiritual displacement and separation from God is Satan's plan for the people of God. The demonic forces I saw were, in fact, symbolic of the present evil that is all around us waiting to devour us. The warning Peter gives to "be alert and of sober mind... Your enemy the devil prowls around like a roaring lion looking for someone to devour" (1 Peter 5:8 NIV) should not be taken for granted. It is of great necessity for you to be watchful, vigilant, and prepared at all time, much like the two warriors were in the dream.

When I yelled out, "Something is wrong" and saw the demons coming towards us with the intent to penetrate the walls to cause harm, one warrior turned on the light and encouraged everyone not to fear. He reassured us that we'd be safe. Please understand this great truth: Darkness cannot penetrate light; therefore, we cannot be destroyed if we are in the light. John went on record declaring that he and the other disciples had witnessed this light and heard of it by Jesus Christ:

> God is light, and in Him is no darkness at all. If we say that we have fellowship with Him, and walk in darkness, we lie, and do not the truth: But if we walk in the light, as He is in the light, we have fellowship one with another and the blood of Jesus Christ His Son cleanseth us from all sin. (1 John 1:5)

A warrior turned on the light. As prepared as the warriors were to fight, to do battle with the enemy, all we had to do was stand in the light. You see, the warrior had power in his understanding of the light. Deuteronomy says, "Israel then shall dwell in safety alone…also his heaven shall drop down dew." (33:28) The warriors knew that their best fight, our best fight, would be fought in the light. We were able to rest in confidence and full assurance that the enemy could not see us nor harm us because we were protected by the very presence of God. My friend, if God is for you, no evil can stand against you because you have the advantage of the light.

Final Thoughts

The mind is the primary source from which life flows. The mind is like an eye; it is an open window for light to flood the soul. That light is dimmed until we come to the knowledge of Jesus Christ as Savior. That knowledge becomes empowerment to reign over darkness. When we began to see God with our mind, our mind is inundated with light. This light, that is God, is foreign to the world of darkness. There is a place of safety for every believer…a guaranteed victory for you and me. The only way to ascertain and lay hold of it is by living in the light.

We say the name of Jesus and fail to realize the weight and power it carries in heaven, earth, and under the earth. If we wish to discover our true selves, we must first begin with the mind. Changing and renewing the mind is paramount. We have to shift our thoughts to begin to see Jesus Christ with our mind's eye. We have to perceive and visualize Jesus, see His heart and His name on us.

Being able to see Christ the way He wants us to see Him is vital. It is the key to your empowerment as you make the quest to find your identity.

The way many view Jesus Christ is filled with inaccuracy and distortions. This is darkness. Apart from viewing Jesus and the power associated with His name wrongly, we miss it altogether because of ignorance (we simply do not know or have understanding). We must ask for and invite the light of God into our lives so we can see Jesus Christ in spirit and in truth. This requires a renewed mind. It is by means of seeing Jesus in truth that you will begin to see yourself in truth, and that truth will make you free. You will be free to be precisely who God created you to be, living out your destiny.

Paul equips believers with the rules of engagement in spiritual warfare. It makes for a climatic conclusion as to how all wars are won which is by bringing every thought, argument, and pretense to the obedience of Christ. (2 Corinthians 10:4-5) Everything in heaven and earth will one day submit to the lordship of Jesus to the glory of the Father. The name of Jesus *presently* has power, and the power of His name is available to us! You will have to fight in this world; it is inevitable. But your best fight, my friend, is in the light of God and in the name of Jesus. We do not have to engage the enemy. All we need to do is rest in the power of understanding. The battle is not fought with weapons made with hands, but with spiritual weapons that were designed for your victory.

The name of Jesus and His light are available to all believers for personal protection and the advancement of the kingdom of God. As I recall the night the Lord spoke to me in prayer, "See My name on you, sow My name, and deed My heart" I did not understand what He was telling me at first, until I began to think about my time serving my elderly uncle as his POA. Now I can share this with you and have confidence in knowing that Jesus has also given you His name and the light of understanding His name—the advantage you need in life.

For every trial you encounter—and every test, temptation, argument, and pretension you face in life—are all rendered powerless in the light and under the name of Jesus Christ. When we do our part to demolish strongholds and bring all contrary thought into the obedience of Christ, we will see victories in our lives like never before. We will experience freedom, peace, joy, and so much more! Before I wrap this up, let me quickly share one more thing with you.

In prayer one night listening to the heart of God for my life, I began to cry out to Him. I told Him I wanted to do all He was asking of me, but I said, *I don't trust myself to be able to do it. I told God, I know my track record . . . I am up today, down tomorrow, inspired one minute but discouraged the next, obedient today but maybe not tomorrow.* Despite the wrestle within my mind, will, and emotion, at my core I wanted to do the will of God. The Lord spoke to me and said, "THERE ARE NO WARS THAT CAN'T BE WON. COME TO ME!"

Please understand, as you read this, I want to encourage you that there are no wars that you cannot win in life! There are no identity crises that cannot be overcome. You can overcome your identity crisis in the light of God. The Lord's name is on you. Speak His name, and legally deed His heart in your life because He loves you. Whatever your struggles are, go to Jesus, seek Him, and get to know Him. Uproot erroneous thoughts that attempt to take up residence in your mind. Pull them down by refusing to entertain them or come into agreement with them. Daily, apply the remedy of scripture by confessing the Word over yourself. Take up your legal right to use the name of Jesus…use it to cover your life and to counter the attacks of the wicked one. Rest in the light, and remember there are no wars that can't be won. You have a winner on the inside of you and that makes you a winner!

CHAPTER THIRTEEN

Change Your Thinking

13
Change Your Thinking

Thinking is simply the process of using thoughts to reflect, reason, and consider things. Our thinking shapes our perceptions and our perceptions shape our reality. Our thinking is formed by the world around us. Our thoughts are fashioned from values and societal norms. Often, the cultural status quo of what is considered socially acceptable becomes our mental default from which we derive all conscious thought. Our thinking is either along the lines of mere perception or reality. Ideally, one's accuracy in perceptions will construct an untainted reality.

It is easy to conflate the two terms and think that our perceptions are, in fact, reality, but that is mostly never the case. Perception is when we interpret and understand words and things in life based on our encounter-experience with them. Reality is "the quality or state of being real"; things as they actually exist.₁ Let me give you an example.

During the first year of my marriage, I was sitting in the garage talking with my husband. We were talking about various things we did and remembered about our childhood. My husband told me he was "miserable" as a child. My heart broke when I heard him say this. I thought to myself, "How sad! He must have really had a painful childhood to admit he was miserable." Later on that year or the next year, we went to my husband's home in Trinidad. After meeting and talking with his mother and brothers, I heard them describe my husband as a child and they said he was miserable.

Based on the context of their discussion, they were saying my husband was always doing something he should not have been doing when he was a child. I thought to myself, now wait a minute! All this time, I've been feeling sorry for him, when in fact he was saying how bad he was as a kid. Based on my upbringing and the meaning associated with being a "miserable" person, to me that meant someone was extremely unhappy, sad, and filled with emotional pain. In my husband's country "miserable" means someone who misbehaves. I interpreted "miserable" as one thing based on my culture and the Trinidadians culture interprets it in an entirely different manner. Was my perception of him being miserable right? Was it reality? Not in this regard. The mental impression from my childhood conveyed a different reality than what my husband experienced or was meaning.

Perception is Reality

It is commonly said and understood in the world of psychology that *perception is reality*. "Your perceptions define your reality, and your behavior is based on what you believe to be real."[2] Our perceptions create what we believe to be truth and it is on the basis of that truth that we live, but sadly, most people's perceptions are flawed. Therefore, what is believed to be reality isn't really reality at all, but rather a warped view of reality. This profound example from the ancient Greek philosopher Epictetus provides more insight:

> Remember that foul words or blows in themselves are no outrage, but your judgment that they are so. So when any one makes you angry, know that it is your own thought that has angered you. Wherefore make it your endeavor not to let your impressions carry you away.[1]

There is a wealth of wisdom here. In essence your impressions or perceptions are thoughts about a matter that determines your reality, which will then determine how you feel and act. My impression of the word "miserable" had me carried away with the weight of emotional stress and piety concerning my husband's childhood. A burden I didn't have to carry. It was my flawed perception that created a distorted reality for me. As this relates to you, if you maintain a distorted perception of who you are, then your true identity will always be flawed. Your perceptions will become problematic, preventing you from living out life as your true self. In life you live and behave in a manner that is consistent with what you believe to be true. So in the "art of war" it becomes crucial to your victory in life that you challenge your impressions-reality in the light of the Word of God.

Perceptions Can Alter Reality

Now that you understand that *perception alters your reality*, you can see how what you perceive or see becomes truth to you. Let's look at the word "perception" a little closer. The root word of perception is "perceived." *To perceive* is to become aware of something, to interpret and understand a thing, to discern or judge something. Our perceptions are the bases from which we view the world around us, how we judge the actions of others, and how we justify our own. Our perceptions define right and wrong, good and bad, justice and injustice. As our thoughts become perceptions, our perception becomes our truth. Distorted perceptions become hindrances and they surface as mental obstacles. The drawback with perceptions becoming reality is that often our perceptions are vague. Therefore, our reality is malformed, and hence it is flawed.

If our perceptions become our reality and our reality is inconsistent with our true self, then you can see how this poses a real crisis of the identity. I'm sure you have felt the pull between the "who" that you think you are, the ideal you (the "you" you think you should be), and the real you—the "you" that you were created to be. The ideal you is just another take on a false perception.

I know what it's like to have an ideal self in mind. The person I thought I should be was a highly perfectionist person. I all but set a law within myself to live by but I could not live up to it. When I broke that law, I felt condemned as if God was condemning me. I share this because many of you unknowingly have established a law within yourself of how you should live and who you should be. I am certain you quickly found that you cannot live up to your own hype. As a result, you are left feeling defeated, frustrated, and condemned.

Perception can be problematic. The "you" that you think you are and your ideal self is not who God says you are. You are so much more than you think you are. You have greatness in you and you were created for greatness. I am confident that many of you have wondered—and even felt—that you were meant for more, but getting there seems insurmountable. The answer to this dilemma is to change your perception, *which will change your reality*. In order to change your reality, you must start with changing your thinking. The mind—not the physical part of you, but the non-physical component of the self that houses all your thoughts—has to be rehabilitated.

Common Thread

I have studied and worked with people for quite some time now. I have worked in the healthcare industry, mental health, ministry, and now in the assisted living industry. Everywhere I go, I see a common thread that is coiled within the tapestry of humanity. The common thread I see is pain, real hurt. As I've interlaced with humanity I have come to feel deeply for those who are distressed as I have sat with the depressed, the suicidal, the homicidal, schizophrenics, meth and crack cocaine addicts, the physically and sexually abused, the misused, the abandoned and forgotten, the aged, and those with Alzheimer's and dementia—essentially the entire gamut of the psychosocial spectrum of hurting people.

I have gone to jail cells to visit with those who have led a life of crime and whose bad choices have led to imprisonment after imprisonment. I have embraced many broken women. I recall one woman who shared with me with intense shame and fear of her future, "I have AIDS," she said. As tears of hopelessness flowed down her face, I embraced her so that she'd know God still loved her. I have watched people come to Christ while others turn and walk away. I often remember one young man I spoke to about salvation, and with agony in his eyes, he refused on the basis that his gang would kill him if he proclaimed Jesus as Lord of his life.

As I recount these instances, I recall a precious older woman in her early 80s who shared how her mother died when she was five. I could still see the little girl in her eyes. That little girl was still hurting, confused, and lonely because she lost her mommy and never understood why. She said, "Why did my mother have to die?" Even at the ripe old age of 80, the pain from her childhood still echoed. The pain I have seen pales in comparison to what the Lord sees. Your sufferings have long reached heaven. You don't have to be a casualty of your crisis.

In this life we can expect to have trials and tribulations. The Word of God clearly states that. However, I believe that much of the hurt, pain, and agony I have encountered and shared with so many can be minimized; and in most cases, even eliminated. What we do, the things we have experienced, our habits, and destructive behaviors often become the identifier of who we are—or who we think we are. The labels the world places on you, the things your family has said to you, the ridicule you experienced as a child in school, or that thing a teacher said you could not do, all have a cumulative effect on who you think you are. Every lie, label, and negative self-talk you rehearse in your mind influences who you think you are. Your pain, your hurt, your failures, your disappointments all become attributes of who you think you are . . . but it's not so! These things are mere perceptions of who you are. Rehabilitate your thinking and you will recover your true identity.

Teachable Moment Through a Vision

One day, I was in my room and the Lord showed me a vision. Now, I have come to understand that dreams are mostly symbolic while visions have a direct meaning. So, I knew it was something very specific that God was trying to communicate with me to share with others. What I saw in the vision was a beautiful backdrop of mountains far off. All of the mountains were flattened across the top. In the vision, I saw Jesus on the cross in the distance in front of the leveled mountains. The vision continued . . . I saw Jesus hanging on the cross a bit closer to me where I could see Him more clearly—but this time there were five others who were hanging on a cross behind Him. The last part of the vision was seeing *only Jesus* hanging on the cross. This time He was on the cross right in front of me—so close I could touch Him, but I could only see Him from the chest up. Jesus showed me His head hanging down with the crown of thorns on His head. Each time I saw Jesus on the cross, I could see rays of gold shining out from His body. The last view I saw of Him was the crown of thorns on His head that reflected rays of gold.

Interpretation of the Vision

After seeing the vision, I was awestruck. I began to inquire about what the Lord was trying to tell me in the vision. With the help of the Holy Spirit, I arrived at this interpretation: The Lord was showing me that He died on the cross, and the cross has four points that represent the east, west, north, and southern parts of the earth. Jesus died for all! The mountains behind Him represent all the obstacles, trials, and temptations that we as men and women encounter. The Lord was saying that He has gone before all of the obstacles you will encounter and leveled them. Jesus' death on the cross has leveled every mountain you will face in life! Life will have its challenges, but for the believer, it was never intended to be difficult. Jesus has flattened your mountains so they cannot stand in your way. He made it possible for you to easily walk above your crisis. This is the inheritance of your salvation. I want you to read a couple of verses and I will finish the interpretation of this vision.

Paul exclaimed, "For just as the suffering of Christ overflows to us, so also through Christ our comfort overflows." (2 Corinthians 1:5) There is purpose in pain that only God can bring comfort out of. Peter stated, "To this you were called, because Christ also suffered for you, leaving you an example, that you should follow in His footsteps." (1 Peter 2:21) Peter also referenced that the authenticity of your faith is more precious than gold and that faith would result in praise and glory at the revelation of Jesus Christ. (1 Peter 1:7) Only God can turn your pain into praise at the revelation of Jesus Christ, because Christ revealed is you concealed. See Him, see you.

I wanted to draw your attention to these scriptures because the Bible tells us that all believers are called to take up their cross and follow Christ. We are invited to partake in the sufferings of Christ. Often, this is the one thing believers flee from. Yet, Christ humbled himself and became obedient unto death, even the death on the cross. (Philippians 2:8) What does this mean for us? It means Christ died more than one way. He died to self (the flesh—his mind, will, and emotions) and he died a spiritual and physical death on the cross. Jesus was always glorifying the Father. John noted the words of Jesus as he said, "By myself I can do nothing . . . I seek not to please myself but him who sent me." (John 5:30 NIV) Jesus Christ was able to walk in the fullness of His identity because He knew that His true identity was in the Father, and so He conceded His will to do the will of the Father. As Jesus stated, "Not my will but your will be done." (Luke 22:42) As a result, now the world has on record all the wonderful things that Jesus has done because while on earth He was able to live out a high level of awareness of His true identity through the knowledge of His Father.

If you choose to partake in the sufferings of Christ, you can be confident that you will also abide in the comfort that is overflowing in Christ. Christ has left you and me an example of how to overcome any identity crisis, how to overcome every obstacle, every trial and temptation. The example given to overcome every identity crisis has less to do with you, and all to do with the work Jesus finished on the cross.

Back to the Vision

The last image I saw in the vision was Jesus up close to me hanging on the cross with His head hanging down and I could see the crown of thorns with rays of gold shining out from it. Jesus was showing me that for every negative thought you have thought about yourself, every label the world has placed on you, the labels put on by others, and even the labels you place on yourself, he has borne them ALL on the cross. You may think you are a loser. Christ says, "Now, it's mine and I take that thought as my own and give you my thoughts in exchange for yours." You may think you are worthless, of no value, inadequate, unattractive, insecure, inferior, weak, flawed, angry, manipulative, low, or just plain no good. You may see yourself as nothing more than an unlovable, screwed-up individual. Whatever you think of yourself or whatever the world thinks of you, Jesus says to you, "I take them all upon myself as my own evil, erroneous thoughts, and now it's on me on the cross." Jesus has provided His loving, pure, good, honorable thoughts for you to think. You are so loved by God. You are accepted by God, approved of by God. You are good enough…you are the apple of His eye! You once deserved death, ruin, decay, even rejection, and all things evil when you were without Christ. Jesus' death on the cross says, "I take it all so you can have all things that are good! I paid the full price for you to have a sound mind, emotional well-being, freedom, eternal life, love, joy, peace, and a close personal relationship with the Father—all things good!"

There Is More

The crown of thorns represents a curse and judgment. Thorns also represent things that rob a person from producing or reproducing that which is good and prevents fruitfulness. Jesus took on every negative thought on the cross. He consumed all negativity in His mind, every evil thought, and every curse that would come from wicked thoughts of mankind. Jesus took on the mind of the old sin nature at its darkest in order that you could have His mind. His thoughts were judged by God the Father at the cross, and His head hung low on the cross so that you could hold your head high before God and in life!

Jesus made this sacrifice so you can come to know and think the thoughts that God the Father thinks of you—thoughts of peace and good plans for your welfare, not thoughts of evil, plans to give you hope and a good future. (Jeremiah 29:11) If you would put your faith in this, put your trust in what Jesus has done for you on the cross, your faith will be to you more precious than the purest of gold. Believe that Jesus has consumed every negative thought, label, lie, and distorted perception known to man in His mind for you and me on the cross. *Believe on what He did.* Renew your mind with this truth so that you can be freed from the erroneous thoughts of who you think you are.

Jesus was conveying that the battlefield has been leveled. There are no mountains that cannot be torn down! There are no strongholds so strong that Jesus cannot rescue you from them. The promise of the Lord recorded in Isaiah states, "I will go before you and will level the mountains; I will break down gates of bronze and cut through bars of iron." (45:2) If you can have faith in this—have faith in his death on the cross and what that brings about for you—there will be no obstacles you cannot overcome. There will be no prison Jesus can't free you from. Have faith in the work He completed on the cross, see Him and believe, and be set free. Overcome your identity crisis through the finished work of Jesus Christ on the cross. Jesus' thoughts are available to you. They will enable you to overcome any identity crisis and discover your true identity. Remember, your behavior, weaknesses, and what you struggle with do not define who you are; the truth is that you have been made a new creation in Christ!

Words of Encouragement

As you read this, I hope you are encouraged and that your faith is increasing. Yet, I know many may be thinking, *This sounds great, but how can I make this relevant in my life?* Let me give you the best example I know. One night recently, I woke up at almost 3 a.m. thinking that it was closer to 6 a.m. I went to the bathroom and thought, *Great! I can get some more sleep before I have to wake up.* However, I felt led of God to go and pray, so I got back out of bed and was rewarded with a wonderful time of prayer and sweet reflection while in the presence of God. Toward the end, my mind started to wander on all sorts of things.

I had a random thought recalling the time I was in college and had dropped out of a literature class because I felt it was boring and I just didn't feel like going to that particular class. One of my classmates saw me on campus and asked where I had been. Having to explain why I dropped the class was embarrassing when my friend couldn't understand why I would do something like that. See, I had to take that class to graduate. (Incidentally, I did complete the course and did well.) But I began to think about how unwise I was at times, and how it was embarrassing to tell my classmate the truth. I felt the sting as if it had just happened. My thoughts had me right back in the year 2002, feeling real shame and humiliation.

When I realized what I was thinking and how the thoughts were making me feel—especially after my fellowship with God was so good—I immediately recognized what my thoughts were doing to my emotional well-being. I started thanking Jesus for dying on the cross for me. I thanked Jesus for taking on all my guilt, shame, and humiliation at the cross. I thanked Jesus for exchanging His mind for mine. I thanked Jesus for loving me enough to die for me. My focus shifted! I was no longer focusing on the negative thoughts Satan was throwing at me to bring accusation, guilt, condemnation, shame, and humiliation. No! Instead, my thoughts were solely on what Jesus had done for me on the cross, and within a few minutes I no longer felt shame or humiliated. I didn't even feel condemned. Get this: Not one time did I say, *Forgive me for not finishing that class, Jesus.* I had asked for forgiveness about this long time ago. No, I simply focused on what Jesus had accomplished for me on the cross and I felt free again. The cloud of condemnation that tried to hover over me was gone!

This is the key, folks. So often, we ask God to forgive us over and over and over for the sins we committed five, ten, fifteen, or even twenty years ago. The first time you asked God to forgive you, He did and chose not to remember it again. "He has removed our sins as far from as the east is from the west." (Psalms 103:12 NLT) "For I will forgive their wickedness and will remember their sins no more." (Hebrews 8:12 NIV) He does this out of love and because He chooses to. So many people are still living under condemnation and tethered to shame from their past. The enemy brings these thoughts up to bring accusation against you, and you allow it.

People will even remind you of your past—the mistakes you made, your fears, your failures, and you allow it. You do not have to be weighed down by a cloud of heaviness and condemnation. You don't have to live in constant torment from your past. You don't have to wallow in guilt and shame. In your heart, see Christ Jesus and the work He finished for you on the cross. If you can believe in that, believe it and begin to thank Him for it. Take from Jesus what He has supplied at the cross. He died so you can live; He became sin so you could become righteous. He took your contrary thoughts so that you can have His mind, a mind that knows the love of God the Father, a mind that knows there is no condemnation to those who are in Christ, a mind that knows there are no mountains that can stand in the way of you overcoming your identity crisis, a mind that will lead you to true life, true freedom, true identity.

Final Words

The life and health of the soul is dependent upon the life and health within each of its members. Arriving at a state of health and stability within the soul starts in the mind (thought process). The soul—which is comprised of the mind, the will, and the emotions—is always being impacted by the world around it, so intentionality becomes extremely important! You must intentionally work to guard and change your thoughts. The Bible calls this the renewing of our mind (Romans 12:2), and one of the ways we do this is through daily reading and meditating on the scriptures. You must intentionally see Christ and His name on you if you are to conquer spiritual powers of darkness—the enemy of your true identity.

As we have discussed the mind in this section, we have to notice how what we think influences the choices we make (affecting our will), and therefore the choices we make which impact our emotions. *You have to be deliberate in your thinking. Your thoughts are the seeds to the type of life you will live.* Your mind's eye is the window to your identity crisis or your identity discovery. I pray that you will see yourself and all that concerns life in the light and through that light, that you may see Christ with your mind's eye. Visualize His heart on you, allow your heart to receive His love for you, see Him, and see His name on you! In doing so, you will gain all authority and control over your life, and you will become firmly established in your identity. By letting this truth inundate your soul-cycle, your thinking will give life to your emotions, and your emotions will give life to your volitions (action/will) continuously. Think it, perceive it, and experience change!

CHAPTER FOURTEEN

Change Your Speaking

14
Change Your Speaking

Speaking is the process by which you use words to express your thoughts and your feelings through what is commonly known as the spoken language. Most people have a cavalier attitude about what they say. I know you have heard people say things like, "What comes up comes out," "I had to get it off my chest," or "I have to keep it real and speak my mind." There was actually a time in my life when I admired people who spoke their mind, because it was something I wished I could do in order to not allow people to think they could say whatever they wanted to say to me. But the truth is, there's not much to be admired about someone who talks a lot and lacks the discipline to speak words that are uplifting, full of life, and encouraging.

You may have heard this saying given by the Greek philosopher Epictetus that "God gave us two ears and one mouth so we can listen twice as much as we talk."[1] James puts it this way, "My dear brothers and sisters, take note of this: Everyone should be quick to listen and slow to speak." (James 1:19 NIV) When we read this, most often we think we should be quick to listen to others before jumping to conclusions, and that is true, but the point I want to make here is that *we should be quick to listen to ourselves as much as we do others.*

We should judge the thoughts that parade through our mind and consider their source before we even utter a word. Remember the old adage, "Sticks and stones may break my bones, but words will never hurt me"? This has got to be one of the biggest lies ever told. The negative things that people say to you become attached to you, things like: *"You will never amount to anything," "You are ugly," "You can't sing," "You're stupid," "It's not good enough," "You're not good enough," "You are the black sheep of the family,"* and other things like, *"You are incapable of being successful," "You are incapable of doing the right thing,"*—and so on. Any of these sound familiar?

I have to admit that I, too, have had people say things to me that stuck with me for years. As I write this, I know you can think of things people have spewed at you that have caused you pain over the years.

The definition by which you define yourself takes shape from these words. It is easy to say don't believe the negative things people say, but truth is, those things leave a mental impression that is hard to shake. "Fernyhough, a professor at Durham University in the U.K., says that inner speech develops alongside of social speech."[2] Basically, we learn how to speak to others based on how we see others speak to us. We also learn how to speak to ourselves based on how we have experienced others speaking to us.

As we learn how to socially engage with others, we simultaneously learn how to talk to ourselves. There are times in the learning process we pickup and start to believe erroneous information. According to research found in *Clocks Inner Speech*, we have on average 4,000 words per minute ruminating in the cycle of self-talk.[2] After you hear yourself say negative things over and over at a rate of 4,000 words per minute, it becomes easy to believe the things your ear hears. The things you say to yourself about who you are become your truth; they become your reality. Lies carried throughout the self-talk cycle become problematic to your well-being. They lie dormant at the onset, and they are hard to detect. When negative views of yourself are awakened, it can be very difficult to put them to bed. These thoughts will alter your perceptions and your altered perceptions will alter the reality of who you really are.

I'm sure some of you reading this have not been able to fully move forward in life because you are still suffering the effects of being wounded early in life by what someone said to you years ago. The pain of those words still takes up residence within you today. While you manage to mask the outside, no one really knows the pain, self-doubt, low-esteem, low self-value, and low self-worth you wrestle with deep down on the inside. The enemy within and the enemies outside yourself will dictate your life if you let them.

People carelessly spout things off all the time and never realize the weight of their words. Words are powerful. They can do wonders, or do a lifetime of harm. Proverbs says that "Death and life are in the power of the tongue: They that love it shall eat the fruit thereof." (Proverbs 10:19) The things you speak to someone can produce death (ruin to their soul) or life (emotional health, wholeness, and well-being). What you say in life matters. What you say to others and what you say to yourself carries tremendous weight. Silence the critics and more importantly, silence the critic within. Surround yourself with people that will speak positive. Speak positive over your own life and see your reality change.

The Power of Words

I was having this conversation with my dad one night as we were driving from North Charlotte back to South Charlotte to my home. We were gazing at the Charlotte skyline and admiring the city. My dad was marveling at what man can do, as far as building tall skyscrapers. I agreed and mused that in the beginning, God created the whole world with His words, and He created man in His own image. Just as God has the ability to create, He gave man the ability to create because we are made in His image. My dad agreed and then told me that most people would think I was crazy for saying that. I can't help but laugh as I write this—but those that know my dad can understand.

However, the truth is this: God did create the world with simply the words spoken from His mouth. The word of His mouth holds great power, and we Christians would attest to this without a second thought. God created you and gave you the same ability to speak and create your world. Your life is in the shape it is in, good or bad, based on the things you have been thinking and speaking over the course of your life. Whether you realize it or not, you are actually forming your world. "Those who guard their lips preserve their lives, but those who speak rashly will come to ruin." (Proverbs 13:3 NIV) A person whose speech is seasoned with words of wisdom and encouragement actually protects, takes care of, and safeguards their lives in every area. Your seasoned speech also helps protect and safeguard the lives of others. On the contrary, those who speak thoughtlessly and in haste create destruction and devastation in their relationships with family, friends, co-workers, church members, and all with whom they cross paths. Indiscreet people generally create ruin in most all aspects of their lives and the lives of others. The fruit of your lips will determine your outcome in life. You are forming your world and shaping your future with the ink strokes of your tongue, so inscribe a good one.

Teachable Moment Through a Vision

I was dreaming one night and as I was waking up out of the dream state, I saw a vision as clear as day. Fully awake at this point, I saw a vision of myself in a room. I was up against a wall and facing the wall. I began to speak words, and out of my mouth came fire; every word I spoke was in the form of sparks of fire. My words penetrated the wall, and on the other side of this wall was another world, a different dimension that exists beyond what we see with our eyes. I knew that this other world was the spiritual realm or the supernatural realm. As my words moved beyond the wall to this other realm, the words that started out as sparks of fire then became explosive, rolling fire! Like always, I inquired of the Lord what this vision meant, and what did He need me to know so that I could share it.

Interpretation of Vision

Facing the wall represented obstacles that we face in life as believers. The wall symbolized obstacles, blockages, and hindrances and can even represent the false perceptions we have of ourselves and the negative self-talk we feed ourselves. The spoken words that came out of my mouth as fire characterized the power and force that come with the words we speak. Our words have the power to penetrate any obstacles, blockages, and hindrances. I define *hindrances* as things that have been placed there by other people. I define *blockages* as things that have been put there by you when you speak negative things over yourself. And I define *obstacles* as things placed in your way by Satan to rob you of truly living the life Jesus died for you to have. So think on that for a moment. Your words have the power to either dismantle every obstacle that keeps you from living the life God has for you, or your words have the power to create a world of chaos. You create your world.

In the vision, the explosiveness of my words was meant to draw attention to the principle that if you and I begin speaking words filled with life, words that build up, encourage, and are filled with purpose, our words will penetrate the spiritual realm and produce that which we intend for them to! Isaiah 55:11 says, "So is my word that goes out from my mouth. It will not return to me empty, but will accomplish what I desire and achieve the purpose for which I sent it." God said His Word will not return to Him void and neither will your words return void. Look at your life right now; it is the product of your words spoken over time. *What you speak about will be what comes about in your life.* Words shape your perceptions, your perceptions shape your reality, your reality will define your purpose, and your purpose becomes the vehicle needed to reach your destiny.

Words Will Accuse or Excuse You

You have to determine what sort of destiny you want to arrive at. In case you are not convinced of the part you play in creating your world and affecting the people around you by the words you say, allow me to ask you a question. Do you know that God takes to heart the things you say? You are created in His image and therefore, like Him, your words are powerful and they carry much weight. Jesus Himself expressed the power of words and how we are responsible and accountable for the things we say. He said, "'I say unto you, that every idle word that men shall speak, they shall give account thereof in the Day of Judgment. For by thy words thou shalt be justified, and by thy words thou shalt be condemned.'" (Matthew 12:36-37 AMP) To put it simply, the Amplified Version basically states that we will be judged for every word we speak here on earth and the totality of those words will cause us to be justified and acquitted (freed from a guilty charge), or condemned and sentenced.

Please take note that in the same sense our words will one day justify us or condemn us before God. In this life our words also justify or condemn us. I see this all the time. Like when people say something and are confronted about it, they deny it, and when proof that what was said is presented their words condemn them. Proverbs says, "You are snared by the words of your mouth." (6:2 NKJV) You can look at any television courtroom show and see the same things happening: people's words are either condemning them or justifying them in the court of law. We must be aware of the traps that come with speaking carelessly. Your words will either excuse you or accuse you. Realizing the gravity of the power and influence your words carry is imperative. Now, can you see the seriousness of words?

Many of you have heard words verbalized of anger, disappointment, rejection, and abuse spoken to you by others. Many have latched onto such words and are carrying within those same feelings of anger, disappointment, rejection, and abuse. You drag this baggage into your present and even your future. Many of you have also been drowning in the pit of your own negative self-talk. You call yourself things like stupid, ugly, fat, no-good, worthless, dumb, fearful, etc.—the negative self-talk perpetuates and the lies becomes your identity. All these words are idle words; they are words of death! If this is what you choose to speak and allow other to speak over your life, then this is what you shall have. Your life will be full of pessimism, gloom, and negative outcomes. Please take a moment to really consider this spiritual principle.

Prevail with Your Words

What you think about, you bring about; what you speak about, you become. Your negative self-talk is self-inflected wounds. If you continue to identify yourself as all these self-deprecating things, a false identity will take form and keep you from experiencing God's best for you. It is essential that you watch the things you say and the things you allow other people to say over your life. Words are shaping your world, one word at a time. If you wish to overcome an identity crisis, you must learn to be slow to speak and sometimes do not speak at all. If your words are contrary to God's best for you, don't say them.

In order to prevail over any identity crisis, you have to learn to speak life, words that are uplifting, active, and productive. You have to get intentional about what you are saying and determine within your heart that you will speak only words that agree with the truth of God's Word over your life. Your words are *active* and *operative* regardless. So make the choice to make the words you speak enthusiastic and full of life!

My Testimony

As you read this book, I know to some I am making an impact and for others, you may think some of this is just fluff. In an effort to show you how sincere of heart I am in sharing this with you I will share my testimony. I don't always do this but if it will help you avoid the pitfalls I encountered on my journey to discovering my identity, then I am willing. My testimony is a testament to my personal identity crisis and how God, over time, blessed me to discover my true self.

As a child, I was confronted with abuse. Everywhere I went, I saw women abused in my life. It terrified me. I saw it so much that I loathed the idea of growing up and having to endure the same. In my mind, I thought abuse was what all women had to endure. I thought it was normal, but this wasn't all I would come to think was the normal.

At the tender age of five, when an older cousin took away my innocence through sexual molestation. I was in a situation that terrified me, but because of what I'd seen around me I feared telling anyone. I thought I would be blamed for it and then punished and rejected because of it. So I kept the secret until I was brave enough to talk about it well into my twenties. After having that encounter more than once, I began to think this form of abuse was also normal.

After having these experiences for some time, something within me would tell me it was wrong. I felt dirty, ashamed, and disgusted. My father taught me karate at a young age for defensive purpose, but my rage caused me to use it for offensive purpose. This somehow allowed me to find the strength to say *NO!* I wasn't going to allow it to continue happening to me. I was young but became convinced that I could hurt this person if I had to.

The sexual abuse and manipulation stopped, but it left me empty and confused. Not only that, I had a lot of anger and rage. The weight of the internal pain caused me to secretly become suicidal. The guilt and shame had me wanting to take my own life. But this wouldn't be all . . . The enemy really had a trap laid for me. At the age of eight, I was introduced to pornography at a cousin's house. It would become an addiction I would wrestle with secretly in shame.

By the age of ten, things were progressively getting worse. I managed to mask my fears, addiction, and pain with humor, fighting, and bad behavior. At school, I was known as the "class clown," but at home, I isolated myself in my room whenever I could. One day, with no notice and no goodbye letter left for anyone, I attempted to take my life. I started taking pills, and after the fifth one, my entire body began to shake uncontrollably. It was disturbing and I had no control over it at all! I wasn't afraid of taking the pills but having my entire body shaking beyond my control prompted me to stop. I put the pills down and began crying out to God for help. At the time, I knew nothing about Jesus, being saved, or how to go about getting saved, even though I grew up Baptist. That day, my life would be preserved by God but I was still incredibly lost and in pain.

Going into my teen years, my body started to change. I became curvy early on. I started to notice that men were looking at my body and lusting after me. I was put in situations time after time, where I actually had to hide myself from older kids who were trying to sleep with me. A friend's dad wanted to sleep with me and I had to run from him. An uncle wanted to sleep with me and he even locked me up with his friend so he could sleep with me, but I managed to get away every time. After going through the excruciating experience of having someone violate my body at a very young age, I refused to let it ever happen again.

By this time, my self-esteem was at rock bottom. Statements like, "You are ugly," "You won't amount to anything," "You are the black sheep of the family," and "You sound like a boy," had been drilled into my soul by the words of others. I tried to be like other people in my family who were good at sports—thinking that if I did something good, I would be loved, accepted, and appreciated, but I was terrible at sports.

In an attempt to look for love, I became promiscuous as a teen. I was looking for love in all the wrong places. I started hanging out with older people, drug dealers, and alcoholics. They accepted me, and it felt good. I would go on to develop the habit of drinking; I binged drank quite a bit. It was only by the grace of God that I didn't become a drug addict after a crazy night when I was holding drugs for a crack cocaine dealer, and had a terrible run-in with his handler the same night. I won't get into all of that, but believe me when I say, it was only the grace of God that kept me from becoming a crack addict.

Oddly enough, one day my brother came home different. He had gotten saved. He was excited about how Jesus had saved his soul. His face was glowing, he was smiling, and he looked happy . . . really happy! I remember saying to myself, *Whatever he has, I want it.* I went to church with him to see him be baptized. When I got to this little church called "Outreach" that met in a house at the time, I felt something I had never felt before; I couldn't explain it, but it felt like I was walking on clouds. That day, I encountered Love for the first time in my life. It was Jesus.

It wasn't long after this that I gave my life to Jesus and my life changed radically. I didn't have the desire to do the things I had been previously doing. I didn't want to hang out with people who were a bad influence in my life. In fact, most things I was doing and feeling in life I was delivered from instantly, like the cursing, getting drunk, partying, desiring to be in a relationship, fighting, and having enmity for those in authority. I was on fire for Jesus. I felt so different on the inside, I wanted to share with people what I had found in Jesus by offering them Jesus as much as possible. People were getting saved, I was hosting a Bible study at school, God was blessing me, and things were great!

Then, I started to experience rejection at every turn. Some of my family started saying I was crazy because of my belief in Jesus. The radical change in me that caused me not to desire to do the things I used to do caused certain family members to label me as some high and mighty religious person who thought that she was better than others. I was persecuted at school for being a Christian. At church, I was rejected by my peers because "I wasn't fun to be around." I was the Jesus freak. I even had moments of rejection at home.

Now, low self-esteem began to haunt me again. All I wanted was to be loved, accepted, and valued. My life was giving me the opposite. As a woman, I felt devalued and incapable of being good enough for anyone. And to top that, there were men still trying to get me to sleep with them, and not willing to see me as a person. I had a relative tell me, "My friends see you and they want you. They can have you if they want you. I have nothing to do with that . . . if they want you they can have you." Can you imagine? Here is my own relative speaking to me as if I had no say-so in the matter, no rule over my body, no worth to be valued. Talk about devaluation. I felt I had neither value nor worth as a human being, much less as a young woman.

It was one devastating blow after blow to my self-esteem. Inevitably, it became easy to fall for a guy who seemed to actually see *me*, want good for me, and encourage me. So, I ended up falling back into promiscuity in my Christian walk. That lifestyle wasn't easy because I felt like the biggest hypocrite. I would cry after the act. I remember crying with this guy saying, *"I was so close to God once! This is wrong . . . How can I get my life right now? Will I ever be used of God again?"* It felt impossible. The guy also started crying one day and told me, *"Go back to your God!"* Oh, how I wanted to, but felt that not even God wanted me.

For over ten years I carried with me so much guilt, shame, disappointment, and hurt from my past. I couldn't escape it. I thought God was mad at me. The feelings gnawed away at me and left me burdened with the weight of always feeling like I had to do something to appease God and make up for the wrong I had done. Despite seeing the goodness of God in my life throughout the years, I still had this hang-up.

I spent my undergrad at Liberty University not dating anyone; this was to ensure myself that I would not have sexual relations with anyone and to protect myself from being hurt. This was also an attempt to repay God somehow. When I met and decided to marry my husband, I thought that this would be the end to all my struggles. I was saying outwardly that I had no expectations, but honestly, I went into my marriage unknowingly filled with unrealistic expectations. I thought that my husband would tell me all of the wonderful things I needed to hear, and finally my self-esteem would somehow miraculously be made whole. I thought he would see me, and love me so tenderly that I would never feel unlovable again. But when I wasn't shown love in the manner I thought

I needed, my world began to fall apart. I became depressed and hopeless.

This was familiar since as a teen I also felt this and experienced an identity crisis. I didn't know who I was anymore, and the onset of another identity crisis began. Talk about having identity issues . . . this was the mother of them all! See, I had brought into my marriage years and years of baggage. I felt I had no self-worth or value as a woman. I felt unattractive, unwanted, unlovable, and rejected by most. The same dark hopelessness set in that I had felt at the age of ten, but this time it just compounded. If it weren't for the belief at this stage in my life that no one should take their own life, I certainly would have.

At the lowest point in my life, I begin to cry out to God again. Overtime, God began to reveal Himself to me, but this time at a greater level. Through the ministry of Joseph Prince, I came to know and understand the finished work of Jesus on the cross and how it is applicable to my life. Slowly, day-by-day, as I began to set my sights on Jesus and His finished work, my life began to change. I started learning that salvation is a free gift provided by God the Father through His Son, and because of my salvation, I now had the grace of God available to me.

Grace is the unmerited, un-earnable love and goodness of God. I began to really understand for the first time that there was nothing I had to do or could do to earn God's love. There was nothing I could do to make God love me more or love me less . . . He simply loves me because He is Love. My thinking began to change! I started to learn that there was no condemnation for those who are in Christ Jesus. I learned that I am free from the law of sin and death. All the guilt, shame, and all my past failures that I was dragging along for years, Jesus had bore on the cross of Calvary for me. He bore it all! As I saw Jesus more and more in my mind's eye and understood this truth, my life went through a transformation from the inside out. As I write this, I've been a Christian for twenty-one years, and I can say my experience in life is one that is filled with true freedom, joy, and hope. I used to wish for God to speak to me and use me like He did when I first got saved, but not anymore. I didn't know then what I know now! I am discovering my true identity in Christ and I desire the same for all believers. Now, I look forward to what God has for me, and how He will use me right here in the present and in the future.

Now, my friends see this change in me and they tell me about it. I am a confident Black woman now. I know I have value and self-worth. I accept myself and for the first time in my Christian life, I feel liberated. I can hold my head high despite my past. Even my speech has changed; I choose to speak what God's Word says about me. I am living on purpose now. This does not exempt me from anything. Life happens. There are days that are blah, just mundane, but somewhere deep down in me, I have hope and an optimistic expectation about my future.

In those late night hours as I cried out to God and decided to trust in Him, my true identity was being formed within me. The Monica of Destiny is taking shape when I choose to believe all that Jesus has provided for me at Calvary. I have found myself! Now, I know exactly who I am. In the subsequent chapter I hope to help you realize who you are. I pray you will never experience another crisis of identity. As for me there isn't an identity crisis anymore, I know my identity is in Christ Jesus and I love it!

Final Words

As you can gather from my testimony, I really did experience my own identity crisis, multiple times actually. I know firsthand what it is like to be plagued by negative thoughts and the ill words spoken by others. I know what it's like to fail and experience disappointment. It was not until I became determined to escape the prison of my mind and take back my life that things began to change. For so long, I walked under a cloud of condemnation thinking that I had to do something to makeup to God for the wrong I had done. Here's the thing: On our best day, on our best behavior, exerting our best efforts; we can never, ever do anything to **earn** God's love. Try as we may, the Word even admonishes us that our righteous deeds are as filthy rags. (Isaiah 64:6; Roman 3:23) Thank God for the blood of Jesus and the finished work of the cross!

Your good works cannot gain acceptance with God, or obtain salvation, or maintain your salvation for that matter. The only labor the Bible tells us to undergo is to "Work to enter His rest."

(Hebrews 4:11) The *Merriam-Webster Collegiate Dictionary* states that "rest" in the verb tense means: "To be free from anxiety and disturbance; to remain confident; to trust." When we enter God's rest, when we trust in Jesus, we rest from our own anxious works and efforts to attain self-righteousness. We stop striving so hard to gain the love, acceptance, and forgiveness of God. By believing in the finished work of Jesus Christ and maintaining right believing, we will live happier, healthy, wholesome lives.

It is my desire that every Christian living in bondage, who is depressed, living under a cloud of condemnation from past mistakes, tormented by labels given by others or one's own self, would be made free through the discovery of your true identity in Christ Jesus. You have lived with your baggage long enough! You have doubted God and lived in unbelief long enough. Your unbelief has made the gospel of no effect in your life. Yet, I can firmly assure you that the gospel of Jesus Christ is still very powerful, full of life, and sufficient to change your life if you will only believe. What you think about, you bring about in life; what you speak about, you will become in life. Learn the art of war. Set your thoughts on things above where Christ is, and speak His words and His thoughts about you. See your life *in Him* and watch yourself break free of all the negative labels, baggage, hurt, pain, guilt, shame, and disappointments that you have carried around. Stop letting life happen, stop surviving and take your life back. Live on purpose as you pursue your identity in Christ.

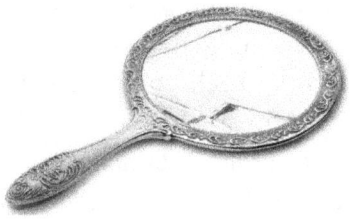

CHAPTER FIFTEEN

Change Your Heart

15
Change Your Heart

I was recently reviewing my progress with this book in an effort to chart my trajectory and give myself a deadline for finishing. It was during that time I felt compelled strongly by the Holy Spirit to put this chapter in the book. What I am about to share with you is so significant and fundamental to any believer who is in search of his or her true identity. I have come to realize that even if God, at some point, has given you a glimpse of what your future life in Him will be like, you will never apprehend it until you understand and obey the teachings in this chapter.

About three to four years ago, I was in one of the biggest spiritual warfare seasons of my life—at least it felt that way. This was at a time I was dealing with personal issues and two family members had gone through a painful divorce. If you have never experienced a divorce between loved ones, realize it is like having a death in the family. As with any death, people grieve. We all deal with death and loss by mourning differently. I will spare the details in an effort to protect all parties involved, but I will say what I witnessed at times, I could never have imagined. So, I made it my mission to help the two individuals carry their burdens while dealing with my own personal issues. I would counsel and advise these two people, while at the same time pray to God in tearful agony on their behalf.

Just when I thought things could not get any worse, I lost my favorite uncle to a heart attack . . . and that wasn't all. I began to hear things being said about me by loved ones that were painful and untrue. When close family members talk about you and you know it is not true, it is a demoralizing and crushing blow to your soul. I felt the sting of emotional devastation. The slander not only hurt me, but my marriage as well. The first thing I wanted to do was protect my character. I wanted to stand on the highest mountaintop and declare my truth and dismantle the lies that were sent by Satan to destroy me. I was deeply hurt.

From these serious wounds, anger began to fester and take root in my soul. My heart was hardening. There were times I felt I would "catch a case" on anyone who approached me wrongly. I nearly became Tyler Perry's Madea—just without the granny suit. I told God I was done! I remember ranting to him, "WHAT IS IT ALL FOR?" "How come when you try to live your life right, love people, and be considerate of others, people turn around and hurt you?!" I know I am certainly not perfect by any means, but one thing I am is loyal and sincere in heart. I was finished with people. I told myself that I was prepared to live in isolation. I was building my walls high, and fortifying them to keep people out and protect myself from being hurt.

I am so grateful that God doesn't dismiss us and turn away when we make foolish declarations of not doing His will when things don't go our way. I made my volitions known to God, all while continuing to go to Him in prayer. One night, my husband and son were out, and I was home alone lying on the couch thinking about everything. I asked Jesus the following questions: "How did you do it? How did you deal with people who were close to you and ended up betraying you?" As I was asking these questions, more questions were ruminating in my mind like: "How could you love them, how could you forgive them?" And in one of the rarest moments in my life, I heard the voice of the Lord speak to me audibly. He said, **"I knew my Father."** That was all He said, nothing more and nothing less—yet, somehow in those few words He spoke came such a powerful illumination of how we are to go about loving and forgiving our neighbor.

Forgiveness Is Love

Jesus was able to forgive because He knew the heart and mind of the Father so well that forgiveness was effortless. He knew that God the Father so loved the world that the Father sent Himself (Jesus) into the world to save all who would believe on Him. Jesus also knew that the Father's intention for sending Him (Jesus) was not to condemn the world. God the Father did not send Jesus to express disapproval of humanity, or to disparage, punish, or pass judgment on humanity. (John 3:16-17) When we forgive, we are actually showing one of the greatest acts of love. Let's take a closer look at what love is:

> Love endures long and is patient and kind; love never is envious nor boils over with jealousy; is not boastful or vainglorious, does not display itself haughtily. It is not conceited (arrogant and inflated with pride); it is not rude (unmannerly) and does not act unbecomingly. Love (God's love in us) does not insist on its own right or its own way, for it is not self-seeking; it is not touchy or fretful or resentful; it takes no account of the evil done to it [it pays no attention to a suffered wrong]. It does not rejoice at injustice and unrighteousness, but rejoices when right and truth prevail. Love bears up under anything and everything that comes and is ever ready to believe the best of every person; its hopes are fadeless under all circumstances, and it endures everything [without weakening]. Love never fails [fades out or becomes obsolete or comes to an end]. (1 Corinthians 13:4-8 AMP)

Love, as Paul describes it, is not what we know it to be in today's vernacular or how it is played out in Hollywood. The type of love we are often familiar with is superficial; love is given based on shallowness of attraction and affection, it is shown based on a give-and-take system, and it is met with conditions. Love is the one thing that all of humanity seeks after in some form or another, but is often the one thing that is rarely obtained or maintained for that matter. Christ-like love takes no account of the injustice it suffers; it does not keep score, but it intentionally chooses to cover any and all injustice.

After having this "aha!" moment with the Lord, I began to do like I always do. I began to ponder. I knew I needed to forgive the injustice I had endured, but I wanted to know why it was so important to forgive. I had always heard that when we forgive, we are doing ourselves a favor by not giving the person who wronged us power over our lives, and we are actually setting ourselves free. I believed that these assertions had truth to them, but I kept feeling like there was more to this that I hadn't yet learned. Forgiveness came easy to me on some occasions, as I am sure the same applies to you. However, I found it hard for me to do in other situations. So, I went to the Bible and began to study what the Word of God had to say about forgiveness.

Forgive Our Debts As We Forgive Our Debtors

Jesus told this parable about a man who had a great debt. His lord was going to have him, his wife, and his children sold to pay for the debt. The man begged for mercy. The man he owed the debt to had compassion on him, and he forgave him of his debt and let him go. This same man who had been forgiven of this great debt later found a man who owed him pennies in comparison to what he owed his lord. He took that man and choked his neck, demanding his money, then he threw the man in prison until he could repay him. People saw what this man did and went and told the man's lord how unmerciful he was to his debtor. The lord became angry. He rebuked the man and threw him in with the torturers in jail until he could repay the debt. (Matthew 18:23-35) Jesus ended this parable by saying that God the Father would do the same to those who would not freely forgive in their heart those that sin against them.

Forgiveness is important to God. I will share with you a few other scriptures because it's necessary to understand forgiveness and how to truly forgive. I believe you will learn something about forgiveness that will be new and empowering for you, so let's begin. Paul wrote to the church in Rome,

> God commendeth His love toward us, in that while we were yet sinners, Christ died for us. Much more then, being now **justified by His blood**, we shall be saved from wrath through Him. For if, when we were enemies, we were **reconciled to God** by the death of His Son, much more, being reconciled, we shall be saved by His life. (Romans 5:8-10)

If you will read on with me, you will see where Paul wrote to the church of Ephesus, "Be ye kind one to another, tenderhearted, forgiving one another, even as **God for Christ's sake hath forgiven you**." (Ephesians 4:32) Paul was encouraging the Ephesians to be compassionate, understanding, and tenderhearted when forgiving someone. He urged that we should freely forgive and be quick to forgive just like God the Father is quick to forgive us through Christ. In 2 Corinthians Paul writes:

> Therefore, if any man be **in Christ**, he is a **new creature**: Old things are passed away; behold, all things are become new. And all things are of **God, who hath reconciled us to Himself by Jesus Christ**, and hath given to us the ministry of reconciliation; that is, that **God was in Christ, reconciling the world unto Himself**, not imputing their trespasses unto them; and hath committed unto us the word of reconciliation. (5:17-19)

Keep following along with me to read a few more scriptures and I will tie it all together. As we continue reading in 2 Corinthians, we see where God made Jesus to be sin for us. Christ was not a sinner; he knew no sin. Yet, God the Father made Him to be sin so that we might become the righteousness of God in Him [Jesus]. (2 Corinthians 5:21) Now, let's read a few verses in Matthew so I can build the conclusion.

In Matthew Peter inquired of the Lord, "How oft shall my brother sin against me, and I forgive him? Till seven times?" Jesus replied, "seven times seventy." (Matthews 18:21-22) So, I asked God and sought for what "seven times seventy" really meant. I multiplied seven times seventy, which is four hundred and ninety. I thought about that for a while. My initial analysis was that there is no way my "brother" can offend me four hundred and ninety times in a day, so maybe Jesus was just expressing the importance of forgiving people, and that we should do so often because that is what children of God are supposed to do. It's just the right thing to do, right? Well, the only thing is, this conclusion did not satisfy my curiosity. I did not believe that Jesus was trying to be ambiguous at all. I believed there was a very specific meaning here and I wanted to unlock the mystery.

Jesus' Instruction on Forgiveness

The revelation was revealed when I looked up what the numbers seven and seventy mean biblically. What I discovered is that

***seven* means spiritual perfection** and ***seventy* means restoration**. So, Jesus' response to Peter's question, "How many times do I forgive my brother that sin against me?" was the following: You should forgive seven (meaning spiritual perfection) times seventy (meaning restoration-reconciliation). In essence, Jesus was telling Peter that: "As important as it was to God the Father to ensure you achieved spiritual perfection through the sacrifice of His only Son, forgive, Peter. As tenacious as the Father's plan of redemption was, and as faithful as He was to being it forth in Me, forgive, dear Peter. As determined as the Father is to complete His plan of redemption for you, forgive. As important as it is to the Father's heart to cover your sins with the righteous eternal blood that will come from My death on the cross, by all means, forgive, Peter. The sacrifice of My life has always been intended to make you righteous, approved, and accepted by the Father, so forgive, Peter. In the face of justice the Father made a legal reformation to have you acquitted of all sin and have you attain spiritual perfection through simply believing on Me (Jesus Christ), I urge you, forgive. As needful as it is for us to live in and walk out of the spiritual perfection freely giving to us by God the Father through Me (Christ), we ought to freely forgive one another, Peter. As intentional as God the Father is to secure your spiritual perfection and restoration to Him, you ought to intentionally forgive your brother continuously every time he offends you, Peter." Jesus' reply to Peter applies to all.

Spiritual Perfection and Restoration

You should forgive seven (meaning *spiritual perfection*) times seventy (meaning *restoration-reconciliation*). With God, everything goes back to love and restoration. We know that the finished work of the cross was the vehicle He chose for us to be reconciled back to Him because He loves us so much. In fact, God the Father celebrated His love toward us while we (the world—all of humanity) were sinners—without a thought of ever loving Him or wanting a relationship with Him. (Roman 5:8) Did you know that the Father was happy to have His Son, Jesus, shed His blood to justify us, to make us righteous, and bring us into right relationship with Him? We see in 2 Corinthians that it was, in fact, God the Father in Christ (personally in Christ, working in and through Christ) who was reconciling the world to himself (5:17-19). From the truth in these scriptures, we get a clear picture of the heart of God and how precious the ministry of reconciliation is to Him. Restoration is the fruit of forgiveness, and both of these are rooted in Love.

You see, when we forgive, we are most like our heavenly Father. He freely forgives us through His Son because it secures our spiritual perfection due to Jesus being perfect. The Father safeguards our restoration because His Son bridged the gap between God and man, and the Father cherishes His relationship with humanity. So when we forgive, we choose spiritual perfection for ourselves and desire it for others. We also agree with God that we are spiritually perfect in Christ. When we forgive, we partner with God in the restoration of humanity to God and to one another. Our restoration gives us harmony with God and others. This is why we are to forgive. And I might add, forgiving yourself has the same requirement. One can conclude that acts of forgiveness is love because it was love that motivated God the Father to forgive humanity in the first place. Love drove God to redeem you, making you spiritually perfect through Christ's perfection. God's love propelled Him to restore you to right relationship with Him, thus qualifying you to be His child, accepted, approved, and beloved by Him.

Now we know, too, that we are made in His image and we are called to be like Him. Since He is love and from Him flows forgiveness and restoration, we are called to be like Him in this. What does love do? Love covers a multitude of sin. (1 Peter 4:8) It does not hold on to or tally up the wrongdoings of others. Jesus taught that we should forgive those who offend us in the heart. It is important to reference the heart because thoughts and painful emotions associated with any offense will still surface after you forgive your offender. The key is to choose to forgive just like you chose to make Jesus Lord of your life. You must choose to forgive in the heart. If you refuse, then God the Father will hold your debts against you.

In forgiving, we are also reminded to be compassionate and understanding toward others, even as the Father for Christ's sake has forgiven us. (Ephesians 4:32) The Father wants us to be love as He is love—as we are His children. (1 John 4:7) It bears repeating:

When we forgive, we are most like our heavenly Father who freely forgives us through His Son. And when we forgive, we partner with God in the restoration of humanity to God and to one another. First John 4:17 sums the subject matter up best: "And as we live in God, our love grows more perfect. So we will not be afraid on the day of judgment, but we can face Him with confidence because we live like Jesus here in this world."

Final Words

To say the least, after learning this I was able to forgive and actively choose to love people still. My heart changed. It was in this moment I chose to take down my walls, let people in, and give of myself wholeheartedly and sincerely so that others may know the love of the Father. I wanted to empower people through the free gift of life and identity in Christ. I realized that forgiveness results in our personal freedom to some extent, but it is not all about us—it is so much more! Our forgiveness shows a sign that we want relationship with others and with God as much as He wants relationship with us.

You will see that as your love for God and others grows, it will be the catalyst from which the wellspring of life, which is love, will come forth. In the "art of war," the rules of engagement is different for the believer. Having a loving heart is a weapon of light and in it the kingdom of darkness cannot stand. Love is at the core of all things good, especially forgiveness, and truly, love is the core of who we are. We are created in His image and we are called to be love, as He is love. (John 13:34) If you will change your heart, your life will also be changed.

SECTION FIVE

Discovering Your True Identity

CHAPTER SIXTEEN

Jesus Christ, Your Example

16
Jesus Christ, Your Example

In my search for identity I often asked God, Who am I? I felt, as I am sure you probably also have at some point in life, that I was meant for more. My life was mundane, yet I felt strongly that there had to be a cure for the commonplace. This "more" I was created for, whatever it was, I wanted it. God spoke to me and said, "I know you want to know who you are, I will show you. Just come to me." He would often remind me to "See me" throughout my quest. We were covering ground. I was slowly learning who I was, but a shift happened one night in prayer. I went from asking Who am I? to Who are you? This was groundbreaking because as I began to see Jesus and come to know who He was, I began to change. Oftentimes, I was not aware of the change taking place on the inside of me. I started thinking different, feeling different, acting different in most areas of my life. As I saw the identity of Jesus Christ, I saw my identity. I was finding myself for the first time in life.

I would like to share with you an interesting fact, one that will be beneficial to your understanding of the law given by Moses and the new law provided through Jesus. Covering this topic is foundational to you understanding your true identity. As you see Jesus in this, I pray you start to see yourself. One day I began to think about the word "stone." Seems random, right? Out of all the things in the world this word came to mind. Did you know that Paul often mentions that the law was written on stones? Every word in the Bible is not only intentionally mentioned by God, but also has hidden meaning tucked away for those who will hunt for it. My inquiry as to what the word "stone" meant in the Bible led me to this bit of information: "Stone" or "rock" in Hebrew is *eban* and it looks like the letters "P" and "X" in English.

אבן

In Hebrew you must read from right to left, as opposed to the English language which reads left to right. The *Aleph*, which is the letter that looks like the "X" to the right, is "the first character in the Hebrew alphabet and represents God or heavenly Father." The Hebrew letter *Bet* combined with *Nun* forms what looks like a "P", and means "Son" in Hebrew, or Jesus Christ."

If we read in Exodus 20, we will see the Ten Commandments—along with other laws that were given…Yet, we note that God told Moses to "Come up to me into the mount . . . I will give thee tablets of stone, and law, and commandments which I have written that thou mayest teach them." (Exodus 24:12) Everything God does is significant and has purpose. God could have used anything on which to write the Ten Commandments. If He wanted, He could have created a piece of sparkling gold parchment, yet He used stone.

Let's visit the meaning of stone in Hebrew to gain some understanding. We start to read the text from right to left with the *Aleph* meaning "God" or "heavenly Father" and the *Bet* and the *Nun* combined meaning Son (or Jesus Christ). The children of Israel would have been privy to this information. When God gave the law (the Ten Commandments), He gave Israel Himself. The Chief Cornerstone and the Rock of Ages gave Himself. The law was founded on the Father and the Son even before creation. The law is one with God, hence the law is God and God is the law.

Our Need for Grace

Since the death of Jesus Christ and His resurrection, we are no longer under the old law but under the new law of grace. Why did we need grace to start with? First of all, when the law was given, God had given man His standards, which were equivalent to God Himself, and what man could truly uphold such a holy law before a just God but God Himself. Yet, the children of Israel insisted that, "All that the LORD commands, we will do." (Exodus 19:8) This was an impossible task for any man! Under the Mosaic Law, when a person failed to uphold or obey one part of the law, he automatically became guilty of the *entire law*. His guilt was worthy of death. That's right! No matter which law you failed to uphold, it was punishable by death.

God, in His mercy, knew that man could not uphold His holy, righteous law. So He made provision for man's sin to be covered through the shedding of innocent blood. Israel needed a high priest to intervene on its behalf to make atonement for sin so that death and curses would be prevented. The shedding of blood of innocent animals was instituted to atone for the sins of the nation. The high priest's mediation made amends and satisfied the wrath of God toward humanity for its sins. The blood of the innocent covers the sins of the guilty.

The animal sacrifices made annually on Yom Kippur, the Jewish holiday called The Day of Atonement, were a foreshadowing of the eternal and perfect sacrifice that was to come. Without the shedding of innocent blood, there is no remission of sins. (Hebrew 9:22) The children of Israel understood this principle. It was through the shedding of the blood of animals that forgiveness (remission) of sin was granted to the nation. For all the children of Israel who kept the law, blessings, God's mercy, and favor was provided, but for all who failed to keep the law, death and curses came. (For more on the blessings and curses that came with the law read Deuteronomy, chapter 28.) The law was and still is holy and no man can attain it. You may ask why God gave the law if He knew man could not uphold it to begin with? Let's explore that question together.

Why the Law Was Given

The law was given so that sin might abound. How could humanity know its lawlessness without the law? The actions and arrogance of the children of Israel asked for it. They witnessed God deliver them out of Egypt with a strong arm, yet they complained and their transgressions persisted. They were offending a holy God and had no clue, so God gave the law. They thought they could do all that the Lord commanded them to do; they were well intended, yet the reply to do all that the Lord commanded was an act of self-righteousness. According to Paul, "The law was our schoolmaster to bring us unto Christ, that we might be justified by faith." (Galatians 3:24) The law was designed to bring mankind into the realization of the seriousness of sin. By contrast, man needed to understand the gravity of the law and its holiness. This enlightenment would bring man to the end of himself where he would understand that it is impossible to be sin-free. Humanity needed to see it is not possible to uphold God's law in its own efforts (doings-actions). What sinful man can stand in the presence of a just God? "We need God," was the realization man needed to come to. The law was given so that man would recognize his need for God.

Our Sins Covered

Now I have to be honest. I have wondered why was it necessary to sacrifice innocent animals to cover the sins of Israel, and could the blood of an animal actually cover sin? If you are honest, there are things about the Bible that you question and some things just seem ludicrous. Thanks to the Holy Spirit, He helped me see that the shed blood of innocent animals alone could not cover the sins of Israel. Israel did come to know that they could not uphold the law so they offered God a sacrifice that would appease Him for a limited time period. However, the sacrifices they offered up were a show of their faith in action. They understood that the stones the law was written on was a representation of the Lawgiver Himself. The *eban* (stones) represented the Heavenly Father providing His Son to humanity for the atonement of sin. The children of Israel were displaying their faith/belief in the promise of the Father to send His Son to shed His innocent blood for the forgiveness of the sins of all of humanity. However, there were no animals holy enough to cleanse the sins of the human race, only the sacrifice of God's only Son could do so. Israel realized that God would honor their faith in His promise of sending His Son into the world to die for the world's sins. They believed in what they could not see; they believed the Word of God and God honored the sacrifices made to atone for Israel's sins.

So you see, the law was designed to be like a mirror where man could behold himself and see his true sinful state. This sinful state of humanity would forever forge an eternal separation between God and humanity which would be an automatic sentence to hell beyond this life. If God did not provide atonement for sins, this state would continue and humanity would be doomed. Atonement for sin is what God did through the death of His Son, Jesus Christ. The resurrection of Jesus was to solidify the fact that the atonement made was acceptable, complete, and finished in the eyes of God the Father.

There would not be a need for another animal sacrifice for sin offerings. Jesus' sacrifice was completed and would be reinforced once and for all (Hebrews 10:1-18 NIV) for those who would believe on Him. Jesus became our mediator. He made atonement for the sins of humanity that would amend and satisfy the wrath of God. His sacrifice annulled the sentence of death, hell, and the grave. Simply put, the law was our teacher to help us learn of our sin and need for Christ. Under the Mosaic Law, we are all guilty and our sins are punishable by death. Under the Old Covenant there had to be shedding of blood to cover the sins of man, but those sacrifices were temporal. Under the new law, a sacrifice for sin is no longer necessary because the blood of the righteous Lawgiver was sufficient for eternity. We are no longer under the old law that ministered death but under a new law that issues grace.

Jesus' Righteousness Makes You Righteous

Jesus came to earth fully human and dwelt among us. He exemplified and upheld the law and never sinned. Jesus suffered and died once, and for all. He traded His righteousness for our unrighteousness. (1 Peter 3:18) His shed blood covers our sin and when God the Father looks at us, He sees the innocent blood of His son; the Father sees righteousness. That's right, the Father sees you as righteous! There is no condemnation for the righteous. Please note this fact: Darkness is light unto God. God knows all and sees all, yet He cannot see past His Son's blood. So, those who are in Christ are reconciled to God through Christ's righteousness.

One day, I was out walking and pondering how, if God is all-knowing (omniscient), if He is everywhere at all times (omnipresent), then surely He can see through Jesus' blood. I believe the Spirit of God gave me this illustration: In a world that is filled with sin, evil, wickedness, and lawlessness, when the blood of the innocent is shed, justice must rise. If God is a just God—and He is—then how could He disregard the blood of the innocent? God would never disregard nor devalue the shed blood of the innocent, so He would never disregard the shed blood of His Son.

This information was instrumental in me coming to know my identity. I had backslidden in my Christian walk. I struggled to understand if God would take me back, or why He would want me back. I rededicated my life back to God years ago but felt so distant and fearful of not earning His love. After seeing that God gave the *eban* (law on stones), He was, in fact, giving Himself to humanity through His Son. Under the old law the stones-law was an extension of humanity. But under the New Covenant agreement, the law no longer exists outside of man but inside man. The man or woman who believes on the Son of God and His sacrifice has the righteous Lawgiver on the inside.

Why is this important? Let me tell you. Hebrews 10:16 (NIV) states, "This is the covenant I will make with them after that time, says the LORD. I will put my laws in their hearts, and I will write them on their minds." For you who believe on Jesus Christ as the Son of God and His sacrifice for sin, God puts His *eban* (law) inside of you. What does this mean? First, you must understand that the stones-law is equal with God the Father, the Son of God is the Lawgiver. Therefore, the stones-law is equal with the Son of God who is the lawful one, the righteous one, the holy one of God. Jesus is the only one who can uphold the righteous, holy law of God the Father. Now after believing on Jesus, the Father places that law—which is Jesus, who is righteous, lawful, and holy—in you. This now makes you one with Christ Jesus—lawful, righteous, and holy unto God the Father.

You must realize that your position as a child of God will never change. Consider this example: Once you are a child of someone, you are always someone's child. Those of you who have children and have parents can understand this fact. You will never be able to stop being your parents' child. Your child cannot stop being your child. So we have to consider the sin factor. Even with sin, child of God, your position has not and will not change. Your condition may change, but your position will never change.

Position vs. Condition

I share this with you because in my quest for identity, fear gripped my life and held me back. I had feared that I could never repay God for the wrong I had done. I carried the failures of my past into my future and it was preventing me from experiencing the best of life. There are teachings in churches that are condoning condemnation. Some preachers teach things like *If you sin, you will be cursed; If you leave this church, you are out of the will of God for your life, hence you will be punished in some regard. If you backslide, you are going to hell. If you do not do what God says, He will use someone else.* God can use someone else but some preachers teach such things as if you are expendable to God. This is not so under the New Covenant of the grace of God.

Under grace we are forgiven and our salvation is secure in Christ. If the sin of Adam made humanity sinful, how much more would the atonement Jesus made make all men righteous who believe on Him? Our righteousness in Christ is secure. This is grace. Where the sins of humanity abound, grace did much more abound. (Romans 5:20) The subject of grace was a large part of Paul's ministry to the world. Paul taught on the grace of God so much that it confused people. They asked him, *Should we continue in sin that grace may abound?* (Roman 6:1) Paul said certainly not! If you sow to your flesh, you will reap things pertaining to sin and the flesh. If you sow to the Spirit of God, you will reap the blessings of God. (Galatians 6:8) It's just that simple.

Teachable Moment Through a Dream

I had been working towards the goal of management for about two years after returning to work from being a stay-at-home mom. Things were shaping up. I made it a point to honor God on my job. After the first year I got a promotion to another department. I enjoyed the job but it was not the position I was working toward. A year later the opportunity came available where I could apply for a management position. Around this time I started focusing on something in my personal life. My mind began to drift. I had thoughts that I should not have been thinking. I started to get a bit hard-hearted and self-centered.

After going on an interview, God confronted me about my thoughts. I proceeded with trying to get into management without dealing with the error of my ways. Then I had a dream. I dreamed I was to meet up with old friends named Kathy and Eddie. I saw Eddie waving at me while driving on the road so I could see where to meet them. I shouted, "I'm coming!" I proceeded to go meet them. I was dragging a bag with me across an open field that had no grass. As I walked through the field, it was making me dirty.

When I reached my destination, I was at the business office of a college waiting to pay for my books so I could start school. They told me I had to wait till next semester because I had no money to pay for my books. I tried to see if there were other alternatives but to no avail. I had no means to pay so I had to wait a semester to proceed.

Dream Interpretation

I felt I knew what the dream meant right away but I asked God anyway. In the dream I was going to meet friends named Kathy and Eddie. Kathy means purity and Eddie means rich, happy, and friendly. God was telling me that I was trying to maintain a lifestyle of purity and friendliness with Him while trying to pursue wealth and happiness in my own efforts. This was displayed in the dream as I tried meeting up with Kathy and Eddie by walking through a dirt field, opposed to walking on the road, which represented the path of righteousness. When I reached my destination, I could not advance because I lacked the resources to do so.

Due to my lack I had to wait the same amount of time as a semester and the break between semesters. God told me that promotion belonged to me and that it was coming, but because I chose not to obey Him when He confronted me about the error of my heart, I had to wait for a period of five to six months.

I wasn't happy about the news. I even avoided God for a few days. I went to work and people were literally hugging me, saying, "Goodbye, Monica, I'm so happy for you. You are going to get this job and do well." I had this happen to me about three different times. It was embarrassing. I went on three different interviews knowing I wasn't going to get the job while sitting in the interview. I had one co-worker say something like, "You need to pray; this must be a sign from God. You are supposed to be doing something spiritual." This was crazy because I never broadcast I was a Christian on my job. I conversed with her saying, "Things will happen in time," secretly knowing the real reason I was still on the job even though the statement was true.

I determined that despite my delay I would still honor God by serving the residents with the same care and sincerity of heart I had always done. And like clockwork, when I was not looking, my executive director approached me about an opportunity that opened up. She informed me that another executive director called to see if I would be interested in the position. Of course, I took advantage of the opportunity.

I share this story of my life and this dream not to impress you, but to impress upon you that God is love and even when he says no, or chooses to delay answers to prayers. I mentioned the fears I used to have because of my past failures. I feared God and progress. My childhood and Christian upbringing had me thinking that God was an angry God. The condemnation of my past sins was suffocating me, preventing me from living. As I learned the truth of God's love and the relationship He secured for me to have with Him through Jesus Christ, I realized God was not an angry God waiting to issue out judgment on those who did wrong. God, however, is still a God of holiness that has a standard of righteousness He expects every believer to adhere to. Yet, lies like the ones I believed have many Christian living in fear of God.

God is not angry, manipulative, or controlling, but religion is. He is not demanding but religion is. God is not about religion but relationship. Religion looks on the outward appearance of man; religion says *if he looks good and is doing well in life, then he is all right*. God, however, looks at the heart of man. He lovingly wants a relationship with you. God is not surprised by your sin or your failures. He has your best interest at heart. Remember, "God sent not His Son into the world to condemn the world, but that the world through Him might be saved. (John 3:17) It is Satan that condemns by bring accusations against you. He draws you away and the consequences of sin wreak havoc. God hates sin because He knows what sin does to you. Sin is enjoyable for a while but leads to brokenness and despair, while right living leads to happiness and fulfillment. This is what God wants for us but He cannot choose it for us. God will do His part to keep His children in the path of righteousness, safe from the snares of sin. The choice is left up to you as to what you want in life.

I feel my dream and testimony can be helpful for you to see the difference in an angry god vs. a loving God who is our Heavenly Father. God did—and does—what any loving Father would do in my life. He teaches me the right way to live so that I can live free and experience the good He has for me. When I get off track He draws me back, even if He needs to discipline me to do so. Is this not what you do for your children? The condemned Monica would have thought God was punishing me for my wrong thinking, but the Monica who knows her God and herself knows that God was continuing to love me even when things were not going how I wanted them.

As sons and daughters of God, you must know that God cares about you, but He chastens those He loves. (Hebrews 12:6-7) Don't accuse God of being someone He is not, and don't take the grace of God for granted. If you sow to the flesh, you will reap of the flesh, but if you sow to the Spirit, you will reap of the Spirit. (Galatians 6:8) The dream was not judgment or a sentence of condemnation. It was a show of God's unrelenting love, and that same unrelenting love belongs to you, my friend. This is why Jesus became sin that you may become the righteousness of God, and He secured your position despite your condition.

Final Words

God has made it possible for man to be righteous through His Son under the new law. Please understand this: Christ did not come to do away with the old law. If he did, he would be denying Himself and the Father. However, Jesus came to fulfill the law and to do by nature what humanity could never do. Then he made it possible for you and me to now do by nature what those under the old law-covenant could not do, and that is to uphold the law. Our lives are a witness to the law that it is righteous, just, and holy because the law is, in fact, Christ Jesus.

Jesus Christ is the express image of God; the thoughts, emotions, and will of the Father revealed to humanity. (Colossians 1:15) This was why Jesus could say, "If you have seen me, you have seen the Father." (John 14:9) God's plan was to send His Son into the world to reveal His heart to a lost world. After Adam and Eve's fall, sin, shame, and fear of God entered the hearts of humanity. Their eyes were opened to their nakedness and they were immediately filled with shame, then they hid from God out of guilt and shame. Guilt, shame, fear, and condemnation have been passed down through the lineage of humanity. After the fall, humanity could no longer see, discern, know, nor understand the love of God the Father.

God, in His justice, cannot tolerate sin because He is holy and righteous. Any sin has to be removed from His presence and punished. This was not the way God wanted to deal with His creation so He had to formulate a plan that would righteously satisfy His judgment and punishment for sin. These verses deserve repeating: "For God [the Father] so loved the world that He gave His only Son that whosoever believes in Him will have everlasting life: For God [the Father] sent not His Son in the world to condemn the world but that the world through Him might be saved." (John 3:16-17) It pleased the Father to offer up His Son, Jesus Christ, because He knew He was righteous and eternal. The righteous blood that Jesus would shed would cover the sins of men who would believe on Him. That covering would **remain** for eternity. Jesus extends Himself to you. See Jesus Christ's unselfish love for you. See Him and be changed. This is another essential key to you discovering your identity.

Handwritten notes:
- How does one gain deeper understanding of their identity
- How does M. explain our Spiritual inheritance 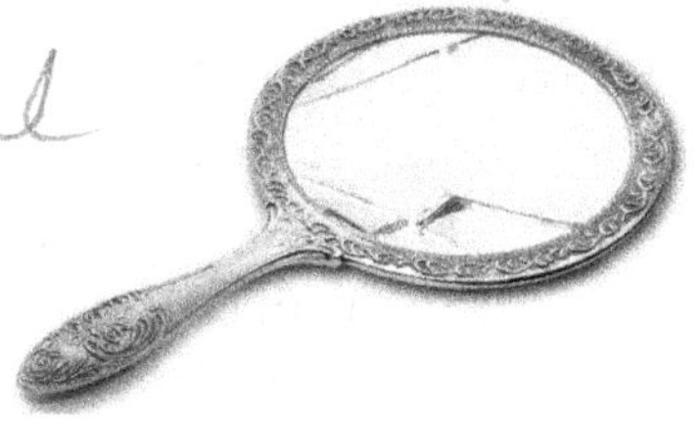
- Do you have a new year

CHAPTER SEVENTEEN

Jesus Christ Realizing His Identity

17
Jesus Christ Realizing His Identity

By now we are all familiar with the fact that Jesus was both fully God and fully man. He was and is the expressed thoughts, emotions, and will of the Father. He is the exact likeness of the unseen God. (Colossians 1:15) God the Father literally created a man and placed Himself in that man. Jesus, the man, had the mind of the Father, the heart of the Father, the feelings of the Father, and the will of the Father abiding on the inside of Him. Jesus was sent into the world by the Father to do the will of the Father—which was to make known the love of the Father to humanity.

In the Old Testament, God the Father sought to make Himself known. He articulated His name about 7,000 times. When Moses encountered God, he asked God, who shall I tell the children of Israel it was that sent me and what should I say His name is? (Exodus 3:13) God's reply was, "I am that I am." We need to take a look at the original translation of this phrase. "I am that I am" translates as Yahuwah which means, "I exist." God the Father was revealing His existence as the one who has always existed, the one who presently exists, and the one who will continue to exist forever.

If you recall, the name of "Jesus" in the Hebrew translates to, "Joshua," and "Joshua" in the original Hebrew/Arabic language translates as "*Yahushua.*" "Joshua" in the Hebrew translation means, "the Lord is Salvation." You can literally see the correlation between God the Father's name (*Yahuwah*) and the Son's name (*Yahushua*). God quite literally placed his name in the name of the Son, and if you reference the original Hebrew to determine the meaning of Yahushua, you would find that it means "Yahuwah saves!"—that is, God the Father saves.

When the angel spoke to Mary and told her that she had found favor with Elohim, or God the Father, and that she would have a child, the angel specifically relayed to Mary that the name the child should be given was the name, "*Yahushua.*" This was a direct word from the Father, because *Yahushua* would save his people from their sin. (Matthew 1:21) So, from the beginning, God the Father declared what it was that Jesus (*Yahushua*) would accomplish on the earth: God the Son came to save the world from sin and make known the intentions of God the Father to restore mankind back to relationship with Himself. Are you seeing what a beautiful picture this is of how God wants us not to hide from Him because of sin, but to run to Him because He loves us?

Making the Connection

I have previously made the point that Jesus embodied the Father. God the Father placed His name on Jesus and put His thoughts, feelings, and will inside Jesus. The moment the Father put His name on Jesus and placed His character in Him, the Father had given Jesus everything He needed for life and godliness. Jesus was given all power and authority to do the will of the Father upon the earth. Sounds familiar? Remember the power of attorney you have been given? Jesus has done for us what God the Father did for Him.

Jesus was and is one with the Father. God the Father is in the Son and the Son is in God the Father. Jesus' life's mission was to make known the Father and to finish the work the Father gave Him to do. Jesus told his disciples, "I am the way, the truth, and the life: no man cometh unto the Father, but by me." (John 14:6) Jesus went on to expound on the fact that they had seen the Father and knew the Father because they had known Him (Jesus). Jesus is the only way men can have access to God the Father. To reject Jesus would mean you are rejecting the thoughts of God the Father, His feelings towards humanity, and His perfect will which is equivalent with His strength of character.

As John takes account of the life and ministry of Jesus, he records:

> He that believeth on me, believeth not on me, but on Him that sent me. And he that seeth me seeth Him that sent me. I am come a light into the world, that whosoever believeth on me should not abide in darkness...He that rejecteth me, and receiveth not my words, hath one

that judgeth him: the word that I have spoken, the same shall judge him in the last day. For I have not spoken of myself: but the Father which sent me, He gave me a commandment, what I should say, and what I should speak. (12:44-49)

Jesus' oration highlighted his oneness with the Father and that he was a mediator, communicating the very thoughts and words of the Father. Jesus was completely man and completely God. He could have chosen to go His own path independent of the will of the Father. He had free will just like we do, but Jesus knew not even the Son of God could live a truly fulfilled life if He'd abandoned the One who knew Him best, the One who created Him.

Jesus declared that only the Father really knew the Son and only the Son really knew the Father. (Matthew 11:27) Jesus executed the will (volitions) of the Father repeatedly in ministry. He said, "I assure you, most solemnly I tell you, the Son is able to do nothing of Himself (of His own accord); but He is able to do only what He see the Father doing, for whatever the Father does is what the Son does in the same way (in His turn)." (John 5:19 AMP) Here we can see Jesus carrying out the actions of God. What Jesus witnessed the Father do, he also did. As a result He carried out the actions (will) of the Father.

There are many examples you can read about during the life and ministry of Jesus where He acknowledged He was nothing without the Father, and that He could do nothing on His own accord. From the time of His childhood up until Jesus started His ministry He grew in His understanding of His Father. Jesus was taught by God the Father who He was. *Jesus' self-image was heightened in awareness because He knew whose He was, who He was, and what He was capable of accomplishing in life because of the life of the Father abiding in Him.* The Father gloriously bore witness that Jesus Christ was, in fact, His Son through every act of love, forgiveness, compassion, healing, and working of miracles Jesus demonstrated. Jesus' life was filled with purpose, destiny, and impact. He lived a fulfilling life even unto death because He was able to realize His true identity through the life of God the Father.

Your Identity Is in Christ Jesus

When we believe on Jesus Christ as our Lord and Savior, we equally believe on the Father. With this in mind we can view the Word of God in a different light. I have used the verse several times, but let's look at it again.

> For God [Yahuwah/the Father] so loved the world that he gave His only begotten Son that whosoever believeth in Him will not perish but have eternal life. For God [Yahuwah/the Father] sent not His Son into the world to condemn the world but that the world through Him [Yahushua/Jesus] might be saved. (John 3:16-17)

Christ Jesus not only purchased our eternal life, He restored our relationship with God the Father. Jesus was successful at doing so because He knew His identity. His purpose was tied to His identity which provided Him with a road map to complete his destiny. Jesus was able to realize and walk in His true identity, and we can, too!

And Jesus not only purchased eternal life for us, but He bore the darkness that blocks our search for identity. His life is the perfect example and road map for us to navigate our paths to discovering our true identity. Your life (your identity) is hidden with Christ in God. (Colossians 3:3) Do you see now why the Father draws all men to Jesus Christ? He is the door we go through to know our heavenly Father and in Him we become restored to the Father. At the point of your conversion, your sins were washed clean with the blood of the Lamb, your spirit came alive, and your soul was redeemed by the eternal blood of Jesus Christ. You now belong to Jesus, and He has placed His name on you like the Father placed His name on Jesus.

The Holy Spirit

Before Jesus was crucified, He shared with His disciples that after He went to be with the Father, a comforter would come. This comforter is the third person of the Godhead, the Holy Spirit! Because Jesus went to be with the Father, the Father sent the Holy Spirit to all those who would believe on Jesus. Jesus told us that the Spirit of Truth would dwell with us and be in us. (John 14:17)

"The Holy Spirit whom the Father will send in My name, He shall teach you all things." (John 14:26) The Holy Spirit is, in fact, the spirit (character) of Jesus Christ.

Now, follow me for a while, this is good . . . In Galatians, the Bible speaks of the fruit of the Spirit: "The fruit of the Spirit is love, joy, peace, longsuffering, gentleness, goodness, faith, meekness, temperance (self-control) . . . If we live in the Spirit, let us also walk in the Spirit." (Galatians 5:22-25) In the Greek, the word for "Spirit" used in Galatians 5:25 translates to "*pneu'ma*." The emphasis in "*pneu'ma*" is personality and character.[3] So essentially, Galatians 5:25 reads: "If we live in the Spirit, let us also walk in the personality and character of the Spirit."

Are you starting to make some connections? We who believe on Jesus Christ and are filled with the Holy Spirit now have His name on us and His Spirit dwelling with us and in us. Jesus has placed His name on you and He has put His Spirit in you. You have, right now, everything you need pertaining to life and godliness through the knowledge of Jesus Christ (2 Peter 1:3) and God the Father, who has called us to become His sons and daughters. You also now have all the power and authority needed to live out of your true identity. Therefore, you have all you need to accomplish the will of God for your life because of the name of God on you and the Spirit of God dwelling within you.

His Life, Your Life

The responsibility we now have is equivalent to Jesus' when He was here on earth. And that is, to get to know Him, just as He grew in relationship with the Father. It was through the enlightenment of the intentions, the heart, personality, and nature of His Father that Jesus came to know so deeply who He was. He walked in absolute peace, purpose, and confidence. We can have this, too! I'm sure you've heard the saying, "The apple doesn't fall far from the tree," or, "Like father, like son." See, part of the key to unlocking your identity is understanding who you are of, and you are of the Father through Jesus Christ.

Final Words

When you get to know the Father, you get to know yourself. When you see Jesus in the fullness of who He is, you see yourself as well—because you are of Him. When you choose to make knowing God and growing in relationship with Him the main pursuit in your life, you come to identify the true you. Relationship with God changes the heart to a point where you become so in love with Him, you will want to surrender everything to Him. You will desire what He desires. You will find a wellspring of spiritual life in the fellowship you have with Christ Jesus and the Father. It will be through relationship with God, not religion, that you will come to know who you are because you are of God and you belong to God.

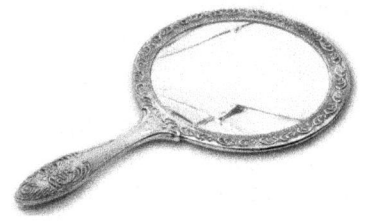

CHAPTER EIGHTEEN

What This Means for You: Your Spiritual Inheritance

18
What This Means for You: Your Spiritual Inheritance

If you have not been taught that you are one with Christ and that your life is in Him, I'm sure the notion may come across as sacrilegious, but I assure you, it's far from it. Everything I have shared with you, I have learned through personal experience, dreams, or visions that the Lord has given me, and all of them are supported by the Word of God. So, the things I share are my way of bearing witness with the One who needs no witness; yet my desire is that the Body of Christ would walk in the same freedom Jesus walked in. I want every believer to experience to the fullest what Jesus has accomplished for us.

Teachable Moment Through a Dream

Before we dive into unpacking what the inheritance is for the believer, I want to share with you another dream I had that was key in revealing the inheritance we have in Christ Jesus. In my dream, I was with some other people and we were discussing supernatural things we were seeing. We were seeing people transition from this world to the next. People were dying and moving on to heaven. The people we watched were of all ages, and they were all believers. In an attempt to catch the phenomenon, we were videotaping these moments with cameras and smartphones.

We watched one man who was bound to a wheelchair. He was elderly and his body was a little crippled, possibly from arthritis. The man's gaze suddenly became fixed—he was seeing openly into the spirit realm! We watched as he became completely captivated, enveloped, and in awe of the supernatural. He began to speak out loud what he was seeing. He began saying things like, "Oh, the love!" "The love of God . . . the love of Jesus . . . His grace!"

While he was seeing into heaven, his understanding was deepening. The experience was affecting his whole being. He was responding to what he was seeing, understanding, and had believed in all his life but now it was being made crystal clear. His whole body began responding to what he was seeing and saying. He went on to say things like, "The cross!"—he understood in that moment what happened for him at the cross of Calvary. He was discovering for the first time the depth of the truth of the finished work of Jesus at the cross. We could tell that he was coming in contact with something extremely powerful.

We watched as this man began to completely transform right before our eyes. The final transformation was his body being changed into a younger body—which happened to be my son, Joshua. This man had changed into my son but still maintained his own identity. In the dream we all knew it was the same man who was crippled, but now he was no longer crippled, bound to a wheelchair, or old. He was so happy, renewed, and energetic. After the completion of his transformation, he literally moved from one location to another in the blink of an eye. In the dream, I had a phone call from someone in South Carolina, and the man was there in the blink of an eye.

Interpretation of a Dream

When we really begin to see, know, and understand all that Christ Jesus has completed and provided for us through His death, burial, and resurrection, the knowledge of these truths will be transformational. This transformation will not be grievous, but life-changing, energetic, and a joyous moment. The elderly man was initially crippled and bound to the wheelchair, but encountering and understanding the love and gifts of God freed him.

His body changed to that of my son, Joshua. Much like the reference to my son's name in previous dreams, the meaning remains consistent. We have learned that "Joshua" in the Hebrew means "*Yahushua*," which means "the Lord is Salvation." When this man saw, encountered, and understood his Savior, he changed into what he saw. He became what he encountered and what he understood in that moment. He became Jesus. At that point he was no longer crippled, no longer bound to a wheelchair. As Jesus is, so was this man in that moment.

The same will be true for you when you encounter and become acquainted with the real love of God and all that He has provided by grace through Jesus Christ. Intimacy with God and holy reverence for Him will release you from the very things that have crippled you in life. The power of every traumatic experience you have lived through, every negative label and hurtful thing spoken over you will be broken, and you will be freed and made whole.

The things that have bound you to a "wheelchair" in life, so to speak, the things that have held you captive and prevented your mobility will not be able to hold you back any longer. You will experience the energy, vigor, and the joy that comes with freedom in Christ. God is wanting to catapult you from a carnal realm to the realm of the supernatural where you will not only enjoy the riches of His goodness, but you may also find yourself doing things that are astounding to all who would look upon your life. When we see, encounter, and get a revelation from the Holy Spirit about what Jesus did for us and who we are in Him, we are transformed from the inside out. We go from simply having knowledge of Jesus to having a personal relationship with Jesus, then becoming like Jesus.

Who Are You?

I mentioned previously that since my personal conversion, on occasions I have shared Christ with others. As I recall one time sharing Jesus Christ with some people in a drug-infested, crime-stricken neighborhood in Lynchburg, Virginia, I literally watched one guy's countenance change right before my eyes. His face started to shine as he heard the gospel and believed on Jesus. This young man, who was a hardened thug, suddenly became childlike. He was literally jumping up and down in the street with joy and excitement at what God had just done on the inside of him. He had encountered love for the first time in his life.

Salvation was never meant to be about head knowledge but a transformational experience that changes us from the inside out. I have experienced many encounters that were a marvel to be a part of. However, even being surrounded by testimonies of people encountering Jesus, I secretly struggled on the inside. I remember after witnessing some of these radical conversions happen in the streets, I would go back to my apartment in Virginia wondering if there was more to life. I hid it well, but I wrestled with the notion of sharing the gospel, when at times, I could not see the good news in the gospel. Many Christian share the same struggle.

I secretly inquired in my heart, "What's so good about the gospel?" I feared that all I did wouldn't be good enough to get me into heaven. I was trying hard to get there but was failing at times, so I doubted on occasions I would make it. I believed I was doing the right thing in sharing the gospel, because Jesus commissioned all believers to go out and share the gospel. On the other hand, I had so many emotional hang-ups that clouded my ability to see the good in the gospel.

For more than a decade I cried out to God, inquiring of Him what was the purpose and meaning in life. I asked God directly, "Who am I?" As promised, God began to show me my true identity. He began to take me on a journey of self-discovery. I realized that part of my inability to understand my identity was due to the fact I didn't really understand God's identity or what He had provided for me through Jesus' death on the cross. I certainly didn't know what I inherited from God through my belief in Jesus.

I had heard different teachings from time to time about our inheritance in Christ, but it still was not registering until I started doing my own research in the Word of God. I truly began seeking God for the answer to the question that perplexed my soul, "Who am I?" When I started asking, "Who are you? Who are you, God?", it was this question that cocooned my transformation. *Knowing God is the key to knowing yourself.* The process of knowing God foundationally consists of knowing what He has done for us and knowing what He has made available to us through Christ.

Heritage of the Believer

I will share with you what our inheritance is in Christ Jesus in a way that helped me begin to see and understand my spiritual heritage. We will never know our true identity apart from Christ. We can never live out that identity if we never know who we are and what we have available to us in this life. It is crucial to know and understand our heritage. Lacking this understanding will keep you from living out the life God intended you to live.

Teachable Moment Through a Dream

Before we get into that, let me share with you another dream I had. One night, I dreamed I was sleeping in my guest room.

There, in the middle of the night, two demons tried to take me in my sleep. I woke up and said, "What are you doing?! You can't take me, I don't belong to you!!" They proceeded to pull on me, one on the left and one on the right, pulling me and attempting to take me with them. I then said, "Jesus!" once loudly. When I spoke the name of Jesus, the two demons were knocked down. When they were knocked down, they looked terrified, but then they quickly got up and moved to cover my mouth to keep me from speaking the name of Jesus again.

Interpretation of the Dream

Here is the thing: You believe that Jesus is God and that Jesus is Savior, but even the demons believe that and they tremble and shudder. (James 2:19) Often, we as Christians know who we belong to. We believe we belong to God, and that is good. But this does not intimidate Satan. It is the child of God who knows what he or she has, which is the power and authority God has given them that demons fear. As long as Satan can keep you in ignorance, he will defeat you. To the child of God who knows he or she has been given power and authority and fails to use it, it is he that Satan also overpowers.

As long as Satan can keep you ignorant, keep you in the dark, and keep your mouth shut, it will be you that he will crush—when you are the one who was meant to crush the head of the enemy! The dream I had revealed a powerful key: it is not enough for us to know that we are saved and to simply believe on God. To truly overcome Satan, we must know the power and authority that has been given to us, and we must use it!

Jesus' Name: Our Heritage

We have already discussed in great detail the name of Jesus a couple of times (see chapter 15) so we will not revisit that topic, but let me lightly touch on a few key points for the sake of learning about our heritage. First, I want you to really get it into your spirit that the name of Jesus belongs to all believers. This is our inheritance.

God the Father gave His Son a name that is above every name. This includes every name in the heavens, in the earth, and under the earth. (Philippians 2:9-11) What this means is that everything and everyone with a name that sets itself above the knowledge of God, and is opposed to the will of God, must submit to the name of Jesus. This includes Satan, his forces, all sickness, disease, poverty, and lack . . . in sum, the entire kingdom of darkness. The bottom line is this: **If it has a name that stands in opposition to God, then it must be subject to the name of Jesus!**

To all who believe on the name of Jesus Christ, He has given you His name. Jesus promised Hs disciples, "Whatever you ask in my name I will do it." (John 14:14) He knew there would come a time when He would no longer be physically on the earth so He gave us this guarantee, "At that time, you won't need to ask Me for anything. I tell you the truth, you will ask the Father directly, and He will grant your request because you used My name." (John 16:23 NLT) Jesus made it abundantly clear that when we bear fruit and ask the Father anything in prayer, it will be done in His name. Nothing is impossible for you, if you believe in His name. His name is your inheritance!

Do you remember the account of Peter and John going to the temple to pray and they came upon a lame man asking for silver and gold? Peter said to him, I don't have any silver or gold, but what I do have, I'll give it to you **in the name of Jesus Christ**; Get up and walk! (Acts 3:1-8) The lame man was instantly healed. Two things are significant here. First, Peter told the man, "I will give you what I have," then he said, "in the name of Jesus." Peter and John had the name of Jesus and they knew it. They also knew the power and authority that came with it! Second, the lame man believed on the name of Jesus after hearing Peter speak it. The significance in this account is the name of Jesus and the power and authority that comes with it.

Do you also remember the account of Jesus sending out seventy-two disciples and they returned with joy saying, "Lord, even the demons submit to us when we use your name." (Luke 10:17 NLT) Jesus informed them of the power and authority they were given when He said, "I have given you authority to trample on snakes and scorpions and to overcome all the power of the enemy; nothing will harm you." (Luke 10:19) So that means that **the same**

power and **authority** that Christ has in His name we have when we profess, believe on, and call on His name.

If you think that is all, it's not. The name of Jesus holds power and authority, but it also embodies everything we need as humans—mentally, emotionally, physically, relationally, and spiritually. God has provided to us through Christ everything we need that pertains to life and godliness. (2 Peter 1:3) We now know that the name of Jesus in the Hebrew is translated as *Yahushua*, which is the same as Joshua, meaning, the Lord is Salvation. Now let's look at the word "salvation" a bit closer to understand what else the name of Jesus provides to us.

The Fullness of Salvation Is Your Inheritance

I want to take you on a study to take a deeper look at the word "salvation" so that we may understand the full benefits of our salvation in Christ Jesus. In the Greek "salvation" translates as *soterion* which means "Saving, bring salvation, defender or defense, **he who embodies this salvation**, or through whom God is about to achieve it, the hope of (future) salvation."[1] I would like to highlight "he who embodies this salvation" because we can connect that specifically to Jesus, as it is He who embodies "this salvation."

All of our spiritual benefits are *in Christ*! In the Greek we also see that salvation translates as *soteria*. *Soteria* gives us three specific facets, three unique benefits, which are all housed within the same word. They are **deliverance, preservation,** and **safety**.

1. Deliverance from the molestation of enemies
2. In an ethical sense, that which concludes to the **soul**'s safety of salvation
    a. Of Messianic salvation
    b. Salvation as the present possession of all true Christians
    c. Future salvation, the sum of benefits and blessings which the Christians, redeemed from all earthly ills, will enjoy after the visible return of Christ from heaven in the consummated and eternal kingdom of God.[2]

Moving onto the Hebrew, there are many words for "salvation" but the first one is Yashuwah (Strong's 3444)—a name I'm sure you're very familiar with by now. The name Yashuwah means:

deliverance, salvation, **welfare** (health, happiness, comfort, security, fortune, protection and safety),₃ **prosperity** (plenty, success, influence and wealth), salvation by God (the Father), **victory** (success in battle, success in overcoming an adversary, difficulty, or overcoming the odds).₄

It's amazing that the very first word included in the definition for *Yashuwah* (salvation) is "deliverance." This is fascinating; the first word for "deliverance" is (again) the translated *Yashuwah*. So, the name itself—*Yashuwah*—is synonymous with "deliverance."

Summing Things Up

So, let's recap what we've discovered so far. Your inheritance consists of your salvation through Christ, provided by God the Father. Your salvation includes your deliverance and your deliverance includes your eternal salvation where you will live forever with God in peace. Your salvation (deliverance) includes your welfare, your health, joy, comfort, protection, deliverance from lack, success, and victory over difficulty, especially Satan your adversary. As stated by Paul,

> For if, while we were enemies to God, we were reconciled to God through the death of His Son, it is much more [certain] now that we are reconciled, that we shall be saved (**daily delivered from sin's dominion**) through His [resurrection] life. (Romans 5:10 AMP)

Your salvation began at your conversion, but it is also a continuation of deliverance throughout your entire life and all of eternity. Your salvation-deliverance is in the name of Jesus. Trust in His name, speak His name! Then stand still and see the salvation of the Lord in your life today and every day after.

Life and Safety Are Your Inheritance

Let's now look at the word "preservation." Preservation in the Hebrew is *michyah* [phonic spelling—mikh-yaw'] which means preservation of life, sustenance (food, fuel, provision, nutrition), recovery, quickening of the flesh (Strong's 4241).₅ You can gather from this definition that it is God's promise to provide for us food that will nourish our body and our spirit. Available to us is the promise of recovery—anything lost or stolen in our lives has to be recovered under the covenant of salvation. Jesus has promised to keep you safe from harm and injury.

Let me share with you how I have seen God's continuous salvation in my life on several occasions. Once, I was robbed by a man at night. After the man took my things, he came back to kidnap me, but I managed to get away! God delivered me from harm. In another incident, I was driving home late one night after getting off work. I didn't realize how tired I was. I fell asleep on the highway; both hands were along my sides. I woke up to find my car turning a curve still in the road. I jumped and grabbed the steering wheel. It terrified me because I had never fallen asleep driving. I went back a few days later to explore where I had fallen asleep. I wanted to know how long I was out and determined it was about three to five minutes. . I do believe in angels and the salvation of the Lord. I share Jacob's sentiment in the Bible when he makes a statement to the effect that God has kept me from harm. I can share more stories, but here is the last one. I was single and living alone. My stove caught on fire. I panicked. I tried to call my mom to see what to put on an oven fire. I couldn't reach her, so I panicked some more. I heard the voice of the Lord tell me to stand still, and within seconds, the fire in my oven went out. I was able to stand still and see the salvation of God right in my kitchen. He saved my life and my money.

These accounts in my life are dramatic, but true. Sometimes you need the salvation of the Lord in small ways. You may need food for lunch and go to work and there is free food for staff. You may need an encouraging word and someone says the nicest thing. You may need energy from being tired and at a moment you don't realize, you feel like you got a second wind. There are times you may see the salvation of God multiple times a day.

The point I want to drive home is that the salvation of the Lord is real and powerful to those who have knowledge of His salvation and believe on it! Most people look at salvation as a one-time occasion that takes place when we first believe on Jesus, but it is so much more. Jesus has promised to keep those whom the Father has given Him. That means His ability to save you over and over again in the manner that you need it is available to you.

Please note you come to know Him as Lord and Savior only once, but for every time you need Him—whether it is for depression, anxiety, addictions, or basic needs such as food and shelter—He is able to save and rescue you time after time. Within the New Covenant reality of salvation, and through the aspect of preservation, we are preserved and sustained with life through Christ for all eternity. At the second coming, God will resurrect us from the dead and glorify us as He did with Jesus. (Romans 8:11) As if this isn't enough, I also found this definition for "preservation" which means to: keep alive, in existence, keep safe from harm, injury, keep up, and keep possession of.$_6$

All these things are your heritage! They belong to you in Christ Jesus. He has promised to keep you and never let you go. Jesus promises us in John 10, "I give them eternal life, and they shall never perish; no one will snatch them out of my hand." (10:28 NIV) When you trust Him with your life on a daily basis, Jesus has promised to save you, deliver you, preserve you, and keep you safe from harm. This is your birthright as a child of God.

Freedom from the Curse of the Law Is Your Inheritance!

Did you know that there were over 600 laws in the Old Testament? The Levitical law given by God through Moses was broken up into three categories: Ceremonial Law, Judicial/Civil Law, and Moral Law. Many of you are familiar with the Ten Commandments, also called the Mosaic Law. These are considered part of the Moral Laws in the Levitical Law. Now, think about this: To break even *one* of any of these 600+ laws would mean certain death because you would be considered guilty of breaking *all* of these laws. That's how it was. Let that sink in for a moment.

In light of this, it's important to consider how our deliverance is not just being rescued from our sin nature, but also from the very severe consequences of sin. Did you know that death was not the only consequence of sin? There were also curses that alighted because of sin. See, when we choose to sin, we give the enemy a legal right to set up camp in our lives. Some of the curses that came because of sin were poverty, illness (physical, emotional, and mental), and spiritual death. You can read about them in Deuteronomy 28.

Jesus Christ has delivered us from the curse of the law and the accuser of the brethren (Satan) by being the perfection the law required. Jesus also imputes His perfection on all who would believe on Him as the Son of God and the Savior of the world. "Christ has redeemed us from the curse of the law by becoming a curse for us." (Galatians 3:13) Most people are aware of the fact that Jesus redeemed us from sin, but that is not the whole truth. You should know that Jesus died to redeem you from the curse of the law; this is your heritage. Jesus' shed blood qualifies you as a full recipient of the blessings and goodness of Father God.

God's Blessings and Promises Are Your Heritage

All of the blessings of God are embodied in your salvation! Let's look at Romans 10:10. We usually consider this verse to be among those that are called the Romans road to salvation for new believers, and it has been instrumental in my witness for years. However, I want to submit to you that this verse is a treasure chest for the believer. It reads, "For it is with your heart that you believe unto righteousness; and with your **mouth** that **confession** is made unto **salvation**." When we believe on Jesus as the Son of God and believe that He died for our salvation, our believing in the heart makes us righteous before God; yet, it is by our confession that we experience the on-going benefits of our salvation.

When life brings sickness, disease, lack, emotional turmoil, rejection, or any affliction, you must confess with your mouth your salvation! This is a key part of spiritual warfare. What you must do is locate the promises of God in His Word and declare with your words that He is your deliverance, your prosperity, health, security, acceptance, and well-being—decree, declare, and believe until you see your breakthrough come. In whatever way you need saving (salvation), in whatever area of life you need rescuing, declare your salvation, then "stand still and see the salvation of the LORD!" (2 Chronicles 20:17)

Your Position as Sons and Daughters Is Your Inheritance

When humanity was subject to the law, the curse of the law made men and women fearful of God. It was always this uneasiness within knowing that at anytime if you broke any one of the 600+ laws, you were automatically guilty of them all and the penalty was punishable by death. The only evasion of death was through the offering of a sin offering (animal sacrifice) provided to atone for the sins committed. Now that Jesus has done this for us, the old law and its penalties was done away with and a new law enacted where men could be saved and the consequence of sin would not be imputed to him. Every person who believes on Jesus Christ and are led by the Spirit of God are now the sons of God. That's right; you and I are sons and daughters of God. If we are then sons and daughter of God, that also makes us heirs of God. Paul also concluded that we are joint heirs with Christ as well as heirs of God. (Romans 8:17)

Consider this: By legal right, whatever your mother and father own, it belongs to you in the event of their death. We are the children of God through Christ because Christ died on the cross, both spiritually and physically, making us His heirs. So it is through His death that we are children of God, and it is through His life that we are heirs of God—entitled to everything He has, everything He did, and still can do. As stated in Romans, "For [the Spirit which] you have now received [is] not a spirit of slavery to put you once more in bondage to fear, but you have received the Spirit of adoption [the Spirit producing sonship] in [the bliss of] which we cry, Abba (Father!) Father!" (Romans 8:15 AMP) God, in His love, desired to restore humanity to Himself through Jesus because He loves humanity and desires a family relationship with us. It was God the Father who orchestrated the plan to draw you close to Him and make you His son or daughter.

The Significance of Being a Child of God

Being a child of God automatically makes you an heir of God's. Paul so eloquently expressed this truth in Romans. We have to be aware that Paul was well versed in laws. He knew Hebrew laws, Greek and Roman laws. Paul was able to convey to the Romans what our inheritance is in Christ through adoption and sonship because he knew how important Roman laws of adoption, family worship, and social traditions were to the people in that day. Adoption as we know it today was nothing like it was in ancient Rome. According to Roman culture of that day, adoption was not about the child but about the family. Worshipping families were the pillars of Roman society.

If a family did not have a son to inherent the family's heritage, they would adopt a son because the men in the family were priests and would offer prayers, offerings, and sacrifices to the Roman gods. Having a son to inherent the inheritance meant preserving the family and the bedrock of Roman society. When someone was adopted in ancient Rome, "the adoptee got a new identity. His old obligations and debts were wiped out, and new obligations were assumed. From the standpoint of the family religion, the adoptee became the same person as the adopter."[7] The significance here is that every son and daughter of God is equivalent with the Son of God—Jesus. Your old self with its sins, mess-ups, and hang-ups are all wiped away through the adoption made possible by belief in Jesus Christ.

Did you know that the word "adoption" means to formally approve someone, formally accept someone, show favor to, embrace and take up someone?[8] The Holy Spirit has come into the hearts of believers and we can now cry Abba, Father! (Galatians 4:5) In today's Jewish and Israeli society children call their fathers "Abba." It means the same as when we call our fathers Dad or Daddy. This is so important to understand. Take this into account: I cannot call your father Daddy as he is not my daddy. I would not have the relationship or the same connection to your dad as you have. You know your dad in a way I will never know him because there is an intimacy there that a stranger can never know.

God has made it possible for us to have an intimate relationship with Him where we can know our Heavenly Father well enough to call Him Daddy! Our Heavenly Father desires family and intimacy in relationships. This is what God the Father has done for you and me. He has approved us, He has accepted us, and He has taken us up and embraced us, and promised to show forth His favor towards us forever!!! You matter to God. You are now and forever good enough, you will always measure up, because you are approved by God, accepted by God, and dearly loved by God your Heavenly Father. What a precious inheritance we have in Christ.

We have peace with God and we are loved by God. We not only have peace with God but also freedom from fear. A child has no need to fear a loving father. We are now children of the Most High God with no need to fear our loving Father. We have a rich inheritance in God in that He will always be there for us and He can meet all our needs according to His riches in glory in Christ Jesus. (Philippians 4:19) Our Father has provided us with His love, goodness, and grace (unmerited favor) through His Son. Through the life of Jesus Christ, the Father supplies an inheritance for us that is both eternal and limitless. According to Roman 8:32, "He who did not withhold or spare [even] His own Son but gave Him up for us all, will He not also with Him freely and graciously give us all [other] things?" (Romans 8:32 AMP)

I know I have only scratched the surface of what it all means for you as it relates to your inheritance in Christ Jesus. Your inheritance is rich and can never fully be unearthed in a lifetime. It is said that even God cannot do it. It's going to take Him all of eternity to show forth His kindness and goodness to us through His Son. And on that note, I hope that I have enlightened you a bit and have whet your appetite enough for you to seek God for yourself to discover your true identity and the richness of your inheritance in Christ Jesus.

CHAPTER NINETEEN

The New You

19
The New You

So often, we look outside ourselves to find the answers to our problems when the resolution is right there on the inside. We look to other people and things to quiet the contentions within, to bring resolve, and be the calm to our storm. The answers to your life's queries are in Christ. All of your needs are supplied in the salvation of your God. I know there have been times that you've felt that you were created for more, or at least wondered if you were created for more, and you are. You can find what it is you were created for and live that life. You can discover your true identity.

Many have taken this quest for identity. It may simply have been named something else like the pursuit of happiness, the search for meaning, or significance. Whatever you call it, the quest starts with you. Once you take responsibility for where you are in life and where you want to go, your journey will begin. Caution, this journey has left many destitute because they have not been able to rise to the pinnacle of self-actualization—which can only be found in Jesus.

Speaking of self-actualization, perhaps you have heard the term tossed around and wondered what it means, as it is not commonly used in everyday speech. Originally, the term came from one of the fathers of modern psychology, Abraham Maslow, but was coined by Kurt Goldstein. Maslow created the popular diagram called "The Hierarchy of Needs." At the top of his pyramid is the level of "self-actualization." Maslow's theory of human motivation correlates to other theories of human development, and his theory asserts that humans are innately inquisitive about who they really are, what their ultimate design or purpose in life is, and then becoming the thing which they discover about themselves.

It is this pattern of inquiry within that motivates people to seek out answers in order to arrive at self-discovery. Ideally, true self-actualization would be the discovery of one's full potential₁, ability to impact society, and to therefore contribute to—and impact—society in some profound way.

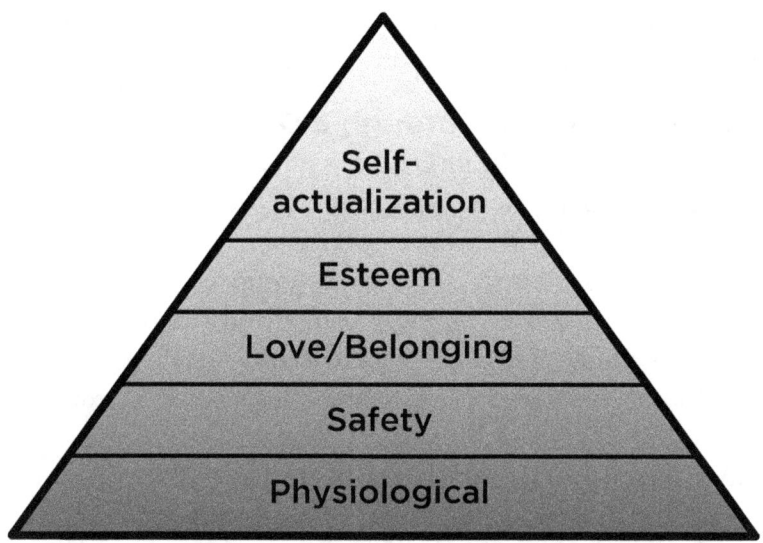

As you look at the diagram,₂ you will see where Maslow lists humanity's basic needs down at the bottom, with the complex needs of humanity at the top. I won't go into much detail here but you can see how physiological needs such as food, water, clothes, and housing are represented as basic human needs. After that are the needs for safety, love, belonging, and self-esteem, which are much deeper needs.

The need for self-actualization is at the top because it involves the discovery of one's uniqueness which has to be done through knowledge and self-awareness, spiritual connection, and the uncapping of one's personal expression of creativity. Maslow believed that humans' need for self-actualization can be reached only when all other needs are met and mastered.₃

Maslow called it self-actualizing, but I call it identity. In any event, you must realize that no one can truly self-actualize outside of Jesus Christ. Who knows creation better then the Creator? No one! Every need Maslow asserted in his "Hierarchy of Needs" is provided for through relationship with Jesus, and through the salvation (deliverance, welfare, prosperity, preservation, safety, and victory) of the Lord. Maslow did, however, make a striking conclusion to his theory, and that was that reaching a state of true self-actualization in society was rare. I agree with this assertion, because so few really come to know their true identity and learn how their identity is rooted and anchored in the life of Jesus Christ.

Teachable Moment Through a Dream

One night as I was dreaming, I was standing on a mountaintop. Below the mountain were two groups of people. The first group was a multitude of people that, all together, formed the shape of the cross of Jesus Christ. The second group was a multitude of people who had gathered on the shoreline and were looking at the cross. It was a huge crowd. Some were leaning on a big rock on the shore. Those who were looking at the cross were spectators of the cross.

In the cross, I saw multitudes of people and they all moved in concert. It looked like they were doing a well-organized dance. Everywhere they moved, they still maintained the cross of Christ. I looked upon them from the mountaintop and marveled at how beautiful the people of God were in the cross. The Lord then allowed me to see what was happening on the mountain as I was standing there. While the people were down on the ocean shore I described, I then saw on the mountain a casket with a man in it. The man appeared to be dead, but then he rose out of the casket! Then another man rose up out of the same body from the casket, then another and another and another. I noticed that every man who rose up out of the casket looked the same. I also noticed that the amount of men rising up out of the casket unto new life were much fewer than those I saw on the ocean shore.

Dream Interpretation

The ocean itself represented a multitude of people. As I looked on the shore, I saw a crowd of people looking upon the cross. These were the spectators, observers, and bystanders. They represented people who hear about Jesus' death on the cross for sinners but never really believe or commit their lives to Him. The multitude of people who made up the cross of Christ represented all the people who are saved—those who believe on the Son of God. I was seeing how many were saved through their belief in the death of the Son of God on the cross. I watched as they gloriously praised and worshipped God for the sacrifice of His Son and the forgiveness of sin. Those people praised God in concert, and it was beautiful to behold.

Up on the mountaintop where I saw men being raised from the dead—and everyone of them looked like the same man—was actually God showing me that when we die to the world, at the point of salvation, we partake in the death of Jesus Christ, hence the people in the cross. What Jesus achieved in His death becomes our benefit, which is that we are saved and have eternal life with God in Christ.

Here is the important fact: the rising up from the dead represented the few men and women of God who will truly experience in this lifetime the newness of life that Christ Jesus died for us to have. There are too few Christians who are not aware that we are dead to sin, the law, its demands, and the fear that comes with failing to keep the law. We who are in Christ are alive in Christ. Galatians says, "I am crucified with Christ: nevertheless I live; ye not I, but Christ liveth in me: and the life which I now live in the flesh I live by the faith of the Son of God, who loved me, and gave Himself for me." (Galatians 2:20)

The men who were rising up out of the casket all looking alike represent the people who realize that they are crucified with Christ and their new life is lived through their faith in Christ. God wants us to mature to the full measure of the statue of Christ. It is the will of the Father that Christ be formed in you and me, so that the life we live will be Christ within. When people see you, they should see and encounter Jesus Christ within you. Rising to this measure is the equivalent of discovering your true identity. Christ within you, your hope of glory is your life—He is your identity.

Final Thoughts

The process of discovering your identity will be unique and will come with its own set of challenges. I don't want you to walk away from this book thinking that the process is instant. For some it may be faster, but for most it is not. I also do not want you to walk away thinking the road to self-actualization is a smooth one. You will come across mountains, valleys, ups and downs along the way with the presence of a real enemy, Satan, who will faithfully work—as he always has—to throw roadblocks in your way in numerous forms. He will try to keep you bound with strongholds. He will try to keep you in the dark, blinded from the truth of who you really are, but remember, you have the advantage. Now you know the art of warfare and have the tools to overcome the wicked one by standing in the light of the Lord. Guard your heart and mind. Refuse to go another day rejecting yourself because you have become use to the rejection of others. Do not believe the ill words of others, but choose to believe the word of the living God

This path to discovering your identity is a progression. Once you understand the truths I have shared in this book, you will experience freedom. When you come to the realization that your true identity is embodied in the life of Christ, you will develop a sense of purpose, meaning, uniqueness, and creativity that will serve as a bridge in society so that others may come to realize their true identities as well. I can vouch for this. I have come to experience a sense of security, confidence, heightened self-awareness, and individuality that I had not known my whole Christian life. Knowing your true identity will feel empowering, yet sobering.

I pray you have been enlightened and encouraged. You are precious—priceless, in fact. You were created for so much more, and the "more" that you were created to be is in Jesus Christ. As I have stated before, knowing your identity is the most priceless possession you will ever have. God has given you the gift of His identity so that makes you invaluable. God has you in mind and He has always had your best interest at heart, even before the foundation of the world. God knew you and predestined you to live a life that is glorious in Christ.

Let me share a quick fact with you before I end. Did you know that the moon does not shine? In fact, in itself, it is not a source of light at all. It is pretty much dark and lifeless. However, it is unique and distinctive. The moon has a purpose that God created it for—which is to separate the night from day and to be a sign of God's providence, to mark seasons, days, and years.(Genesis 1:14 AMP). However, "the moon shines because its surface reflects light from the sun."₄ I like to call the moon an image bearer, a reflector of light and so are you. When you and I look at the moon, we see a beautiful, radiant, luminous white light. You see, the moon has an identity and that identity is realized in the light of the sun. You and I can see and identify the moon when we see it reflecting the sun's light at night.

The moon is much like the life of the believer. Without Christ, we exist as beings that are created in the image of God with uniqueness and distinctiveness. However, we can never fully excavate our true identity outside of Christ. In Christ we can. We not only have life in Christ, we have within us substance that will allow us to reflect light as the light of the Son of God shines on us. It is my prayer that you become like the moon.

May you be a bright reflection of the light of Jesus Christ. May your life reflect the very life of Jesus Christ and you come to bear His image. May the light of the Father remove the darkness the enemy has tried to cast over your life. As you stand in the light, may all trauma, pain, failure, disappointment, negative labels placed on you by others, and the myriad strongholds the enemy has set up to prevent you from discovering your true identity be dissolved. May the light of Jesus Christ be the proof and the truth you need to be set free. May you find yourself standing in the rays of the Son of God, your true identity, so that all who may look upon you see the beauty and radiant, luminous light of your true self. God bless you. Thanks for reading my book. Know that I love you, and most of all, the God of Heaven really loves you! Now go . . . discover your true identity, for your identity is Christ!

Prayer of Salvation

Have you ever made Jesus your Lord and Savior? If not, and you would like to, pray this simple prayer and start a new life of true self-discovery in Christ today!

Dear God,

    I come to you in the name of Jesus, admitting that I am a sinner in need of a savior. I believe that Jesus is the Son of God sent into the world to die for sinful men. I ask that you forgive me of my sins. Come into my life and cleanse my heart. I confess that after Jesus' death on the cross, God the Father raised Him from the dead. I believe with my heart and confess with my mouth that Jesus is now the Savior and Lord of my life. I pray and ask these things in Jesus name; Amen.

If you prayed this prayer and made Jesus Christ Lord of your life after reading this book, I would love to hear from you. Email me about your experience at mewickram80@gmail.com and put in the subject box: The Identity Crisis.

If this book has touched your life in some way, I would also love to hear from you. Feel free to email me. For booking speaking engagements; you may also email me at mewickram80@gmail.com. Please put in the subject box: The Identity Crisis. Look forward to hearing from you. Thank you and may God bless you!

APPENDIX

Dream and Visions Interpretation Guide

Appendix
Dreams and Visions
Interpretation Guide

The reason I am providing this Dreams and Visions Interpretation Guide is referenced in the Introduction, so please review that again. First, begin all dream interpretation with prayer. Seek God first about what He is trying to communicate to you through your dreams and visions. Go to the Word of God when trying to get understanding of details in your dream, such as meanings of numbers, colors, time of day, and so on. God uses a lot of symbolism in His Word and great truths are hidden in the symbolism if we are willing to seek Him out for the meaning. For those who will seek to understand symbolism in God's Word and through the revelation of the Holy Spirit on dreams, it is promised that God will reward you openly. Dream and vision interpretation can be simple and other times complex. There is no one cut-and-dry way to interpret dreams and visions. We have to be led by the Lord.

The meanings of symbols in this Dreams and Visions Guide I have learned over time. They are a compilation of the meaning of actual things or symbolisms I have had in my dreams and visions. Some I have learned through interpreting other people's dreams and visions through the help of the Holy Spirit and the Word of God. The reference section in this book can also provide other resources I have used. Symbols can vary in meaning from one dream to the next and from one person to the next. This is why it is important to seek God first for the meaning to your dreams.

Before listing the meanings of dream symbols, let me first say that there are three types of dreams—divine, soulish or natural, and demonic. The first step that you should take before even trying to interpret your dream is to discern the source! It is crucial to always inquire of the Holy Spirit and discern the source of your dream. Divine or Heavenly dreams from God or the angelic are designed to relay a message to you for the purpose of direction, edification, or prophecy. Your dream may also reveal something to you that is going to happen in the future.

Soulish or natural dreams come out of your subconscious mind as a result of what you have been thinking about, desiring, entertaining yourself with—as well as your personal experiences. Soulish dreams or fleshly dreams bear no significance, but demonic dreams will always bear the telltale mark of the one they came from—our adversary. We know that his intent is to kill, steal, and destroy. So, you'll know that is where the dream came from if it robs you of your peace, or generally leaves you with an uneasy, icky feeling. My intent here is not to instruct you on how to do spiritual warfare concerning demonic dreams, but rather to shine the light on meanings of common elements in God-dreams.

When using this key, please bear in mind that all interpretation comes from the Holy Spirit. There is no one way to interpret all dreams. God will often use symbolism and relatable experiences because he knows how you, uniquely, will understand something and how you relate to the world around you. So, keep this in mind. God didn't mean for it to be difficult or arduous. I pray that the following guide will serve as a set of tools that God will use in helping you to learn how to understand the spiritual language of dreams and visions so you can better communicate with Him and move forward with all that He has for you.

Now, after you have discerned the source of your dream, the next thing you'll want to do is to make a note of what you have dreamed. There are different ways to record your dream. You can write it down on paper, you can make a note of it using your smartphone, or you can voice record it—also using your smartphone or with a voice recorder. There are various voice recorder smartphone apps you can download for free. Personally, I have learned that the meat of the message is often hidden in the details, so most of the time I write my dreams down, but I do find using my phone to record is convenient.

When noting your dream, try to remember the emotions or feel of the dream. How did the dream itself feel? For example, was it peaceful or foreboding? Simply take note of that; don't try to gauge or judge whether the feel of the dream is "good" or "bad."

Also, what emotions did you personally experience in the dream? Were there different points where you were surprised, sad, happy, confused, disappointed, or frustrated? Identifying emotions is very important concerning dream interpretation. Being able to identify with an emotion you actually felt and/or feeling presently is typically a message from God for you to know now or relates to a current event in your life. Feelings that you cannot identify with—and seem like something you would not usually do or feel typically—are prophetic dreams and visions. If any of this is helpful and interests you, other Christian resources on dream interpretation are available.

Dream Symbols

A

Airplanes—Person and their life or ministry

Airplanes (crashing)—People failing, falling short spiritually, people or person out of control

Arrows/Darts—Accusations, temptation, feeling of guilt and condemnation, or trial brought on by your adversary, the devil

B

Baby—Something you are going to give birth to, something you are going to have to nurture until it grows, or it could be simply that you are going to have a baby

Bed—Represents your secret place, things you hold secret, private matters of the heart, intimacy, or sexuality

Blood—Sacrificial blood of Jesus Christ, life, purification, redemption, restoration, or cleansing and covering

Bread—Word of God, spiritual food, Body of Christ, sustainer of life, or Bread of Life which is Jesus

Bridge—Can mean leaving one place or stage in life and crossing over on to another, can be bridging the gap between two things, or leaving something behind and progressing towards something else

C

Car—Represents your life, your ideologies/world view at the present time in your life, or your ministry

Car (accident or on the verge of an accident)—Represents your life being out of control, could be a warning dream that you may come close to or will be in an accident

Cave—Hiding place, safe place, shelter

Children—Having childlike faith

Children (standing happily around a strange man)—How we should approach Jesus as children full of faith

Cloudy—Trial(s) coming, problem on the horizon, or trouble

Couch (lying on couch)—Represents temptation, sexual sins of adultery, fornication, masturbation, incest, sexual abuse

Cover/blanket (put over you)—Jesus' covering, God's protection

D

Day—Newness, hope, children of the light/God

Dead people—The meaning of the dead person's name could be significant, so note who it is and find out the meaning of their name. It could mean that you will have issues with the side of the family that the dead family member represented in your dream

Death (you die after being attacked)—Representative of how the enemy comes to steal, kill, and destroy you

Demons—Evil spirits, Satan's messengers sent to attack you

Dog(s)—Friendly person, or someone who posed as a friendly person

Dog(s) (dogs attacking you)—Friend(s) turning on you, someone becoming your enemy

Door—Access to something, entry point

Door (open door)—Opportunity opening up for you, letting God in, entrance to God/heaven

Door (closed door)—Protection due to something being kept out of your life, could also mean a missed opportunity

Dust—Symbolic of the dead things of the world, could be symbolic of poverty, or humility, repentance and lowliness (Genesis 18:27)

E
Egypt—Bondage, idolatry

Emotions—The key is to note how you feel in a dream or how others in the dream feel, this will provide you insight to meaning of dream

Eyes—Note if good or bad/pleasant or unpleasant, could represent the eyes of the Lord, or evil eyes on you or watching you

F
Faceless man—Represents God, Jesus, and the Holy Spirit

Father (not your real father)—Represents heavenly Father

Feet—See Themes/Body parts

Feet (Jesus' Feet)—A place of grace, a place of humility, a place of worship

Fire—Holy Spirit, purifying, refining, consuming, or it could mean something will catch on fire

Fish—People, God's people

Dreams and Visions Interpretation Guide

Fish (fish out of water)—Not in the right environment (could mean spiritual or actual environment in day-to-day life)

Flying (you flying a plane or other flying)—You will be put in a high position, people you hold in high regard, spiritual people living spiritually, being used in ministry and in the gifting and talent of God

Funeral/lying in a casket—Spiritual death

H

Hands—Your work, the means by which you create wealth or bring in income, clean your hands, or unclean hands

Hands (open)—Provision

Hands (closed)—No provision

Hair (long hair or hair growing)—Crown of glory, beauty, and confidence

Hair (unwanted haircut, surprised haircut, hair failing out)—You are lacking confidence in life, or will be placed in a situation where you may lack confidence

Gray Hair—Wisdom

Horn—Power

House—Represents your personal life, ideologies, and ways of viewing the world

House (white house)—Bride of Christ

House (black or dark house)—Spiritual darkness, spiritual famine, people in the house represent ideologies that are worldly, or people in the house represent holding on to doctrine that is of the old wineskin

House (family house/the place you grew up in)—You are having/dealing with family issues, wrestling with something from your past or some issue acquired during childhood, generational issues

House (dilapidated house)—Ideologies and ways of viewing the world and/or spiritual things that are wrong, deceptive

J
Jail—Bondage, captivity

L
Light—God's glory, God's protection, truth, purity, illumination

M
Mirror/glass—Reflection of the Word of God in your life, making introspection

Moon—Could represent a woman; Light bearer, or lifeless, without light and life

Mountains—Obstacles

N
Night—Judgment, spiritual darkness, under the cover of hiddenness

O
Oil—Holy Spirit, anointing, supply

P
Parents (Both)—Represents a decision you need to make that will need to be balanced: Father represents rational, logical problem solvers, Mother represents emotional warmth, care, and nurturing. Your decision will have to consider both your rational side and emotional side in order to make a decision that is right and balanced

Path and/or road—Where you are going in life, a path you have to take in life, path of righteousness, your life's journey. Be sure to note: Is the road or path straight, winding, clear, blocked, rocky, paved, a dirt path, narrow, wide, or a crossroad? This will help you interpret you dream

Path or road before you—Is your future, a road behind you is your past (dreaming of a road may be symbolic of where you are in your life and how you are progressing or digressing (regressing???) in life)

Phone call—Could be the call of God on your life, a call to provide instruction, direction for life. If negative in meaning, can mean the enemy is trying to disrupt the call of God on your life

R

Rain—God's supply, could also conversely represent troubled times

Road—please refer to path

Robe—Covered in righteousness, authority

Rock and/or Stone—Jesus Christ, the law given by Moses, (Jesus who is the law/Word and the only man to uphold the law because he and the law/Word are one)

S

Salt—Preserver, savior, keeper

Sanctuary—God's plan or work in your life (can be current or future plans), message from heaven

School (dreaming you are back in school)—There is something in your past you need to learn from and overcome

School (dreaming you are taking a test)—You have to learn/overcome a thing that's keeping you from moving forward

School (dreaming you are not prepared for the test while taking test)—You are not prepared in life, you have not gotten what is needed to overcome the thing(s) that is keeping you from progress/your destiny

School (missed taking test and/or late for class)—Not prepared in life, not prepared for the next level but will be tested again before you can move forward in life

School (in college and starting a new semester)—You are ready to advance, progress, you are moving into another dimension in life and/or spiritually

School (in college having to wait till next semester to continue school)—You are lacking what's needed to advance, you are not prepared, you have not learned what is needed for life and/or your spiritual life, you have to wait for promotion due to a lack of preparedness

Sea—Multitude of people, their ideologies, and/or their influence, also see *water

Seashore—You are facing or are going to face people, their opinions, or influence; you are being faced with a choice where you will have to choose God's way or the world's way; can also mean you will be traveling to the sea

Ship—A vessel that houses a large group of people where you may be confronted with their philosophies, doctrine, ideologies, or way of life

Shoes (sandals)—Represents wealth, appropriate attire, can be an encouragement to put on the part of the armor of God that deals with the gospel (shod with the preparation of the gospel)

Signet Ring—You are given authority, power, rulership, royal position of authority given to you by God

Signet Ring (letter sealed with the ring)—What is stated on the letter is final and no man can change it or go against it

Sky—Heavenly or spiritual realm

Sky (cloudy dark sky)—Represents a spiritual attack is coming (could be coming to you, a group of people, a nation, etc.)

Sky (storms)—Could represent a spiritual attack, or a real-life storm that will impact your life (could be financial storm, death of a loved one, etc.)

Soldiers—Can mean saints of God, or angels. Could also conversely represent demons or demonic activity

Stage (singing on stage)—You will sing or God is calling you to do something with music

Stage (speaking on stage)—You will have to give a speech, or God is calling you in some capacity to speak, e.g. speak or preach

*Stage—see **Theater**

Stairway (moving upstairs)—Progressing, moving towards God

Stairway (moving downstairs)—Digressing(regressing??), backsliding, moving away from God

Stairway (moving up and downstairs)—Unstable in life, unhealthy pattern of moving towards God and moving away from God

Star(s)—Angels, light bearers, descendants of Abraham, children of God

*Stone—See **rock**

Sun—Could represent a man; Light, brightness; source of life, which is Jesus

Sword—The Word of God—your weapon against the enemy

T

Theater (watching a show)—Watching others live their dreams or live out the call of God on their lives

Theater (you called on stage)—God is calling you out of the shadows/background and putting you in center stage/forefront to use you in some capacity

Teeth (showing)—Confidence

Teeth (spreading or falling out)—Loss of confidence, losing control, may experience shame/embracement

Teeth (wisdom teeth falling out)—Lacking wisdom in an area of your life

*****Temple**—See **church**

Toilet (using the toilet)—God is trying to, going to, or is cleansing your insides—getting rid of the "toxins" that are not good for the spiritual body

Toilet (using it in front of people)—You are going to be in a situation in which you will feel vulnerable in front of people

Tornado—Something is about to be uprooted in your life (could be an emotional attack, physical/health, financial attack, or spiritual attack)

Train/Train tracks—Could mean you are going to be traveling or taking a trip

Tree—Life, stability, strength

Tree (branch)—Encouragement or admonishment to abide in the true vine, which is Jesus Christ; could also conversely represent being barren/unfruitful

U
Underground (living or dwelling underground)—Dwelling in safety, place of safety, refuge

V
*****Vehicle**—See **car**

Vehicle (large one)—The meaning is tied to you being involved with other people/group of people

Vehicle (small one)—Involves you (note who is in vehicle with you)

W

Water—People, or multitudes of people, nations

Water—People in unrest, the philosophies of people trying to influence you

Water (Tsunami)—People are upset, people upset with or attacking you, people in unrest

Window—Prophetic vision, word or revelation from God about a current or future state, being able to see into a situation and gain knowledge or wisdom

Wolves—People who are not who they say they are, deception, a person/people deceiving you.

Themes

Colors

Red—Blood of Jesus, sacrifice, covering, purification, suffering

Green—Growth, prosperity, wealth

Green (olive green)—Represents oil, anointing, anointing oil

Blue—Heaven, heavenly

Light Blue—The supernatural realm

Dark Blue—Royal

Teal/Aqua—Devotion, healing, trustworthiness

Purple—Royalty, kingship, prosperity, wealth

Brown—The flesh, or conversely humility, also can mean man/the natural

Multicolored—Favor of God

Gold—Represents deity/God, pure, tried and tested to be pure, kingship, kingdom glory

Silver—Redemption, the cost of a soul, regaining possession of someone through a purchase (Amos 2:6)

White—Pure, purity, clean, cleansed, righteousness

Black—Spiritual death, ignorance, famine

Numbers

1—God, Genesis 1:1; 1John 5:7

2—Positive meaning is witness, (a witness of two was needed to verify the truth) Matthew 18:16, Negative meaning is division

3—Represents the Trinity (Father, Son, Holy Spirit), or completion

4—Represents creation day where light was created to divide light from the day, and to specify time and seasons. So "4" represents light or humanity, creativity, the 4 directions (north, south, east, west), or the 4 seasons (winter, summer, spring, fall) [Genesis 1:14-19]

5—Grace (5 in Hebrew is pronounced khah-mehsh, which means God's grace)

6—Man, human effort

7—Spiritual perfection

8—New beginnings

10—Divine order, or abundant life [John 10:10]

11—Disorder, confusion

12—The government of God, government presiding over the Body of Christ, order

15—Completion of God's grace (3x5)

25—Grace upon grace (5x5)

40—Time of testing and trials

41—Deliverance from trial/s, victory over trials/test

50—Move of the Holy Spirit, freedom (Jubilee)

70—Restoration (Israel was restored to the Promised Land 70 years after captivity)

490—Represents a constantly forgiving heart (7x70)

Directions
North—Towards God, moving towards God

South—Away from God, moving away from, backsliding

East—Facing towards God, newness

West—Moving or facing away from God, backsliding, end of an age, the evening (the sun sets in the west)

Up—Moving towards God, progressing

Down—Moving away from God, digressing (regressing??), backsliding, turning back to former things

Side-to-Side—Out of control, straddling the fence, unstable

Looking Back—Looking in the past

Looking Forward—Looking ahead, looking to future toward progress/positive change

Animals
Ant—Diligent, wise, initiator

Dog—Friend, friendly

Dog (attacking or vicious)—Friend(s) turning on you, or have done wrong to you

Wolves—Deceivers, people who are not who they say they are, false teachers

Lion—Lion of Judah, symbolic of Jesus, can also mean Satan your adversary [1 Peter 5:8]

Sheep—Follower of Jesus, children of God, innocent, prone to wander

Fish—Represents follower of Jesus, or the lost that need to be saved (souls of men)

Eagle—Rising above

Bear—Evil man, cruel person

Locust—Destructive, cursed

Cankerworm—Destructive

Rooster—Early riser, warning, reminder

Dove—Holy Spirit

Owl—Wise or wisdom, conversely can mean witchcraft or spiritual darkness

Bat—Spiritual darkness, in spiritual darkness, defiled

Snake/serpent—Satan, evil spirit, evil person, deception

Spider/s—Witchcraft, control or manipulation

Material/Metals
***Silver**—See colors

***Gold**—See colors

Clay—Weakness, common, material molded by God [Job 13:12, Isaiah 64:8]

Bronze—Sin, disobedience

Wood—Humanity, curse

Brick—Man's efforts, false worship,

Iron—Strength, crushing, inflexible

Body Parts

Head—Thoughts, mindset, imaginations, Christ being the head of the Church

Hair—Your glory

Hair (gray)—Wisdom

Ear—Entrance to the soul, where faith or fear enters, spiritual hearing

Eyes—Window and/or light to the soul, vision

Belly/Stomach—Seat of your affections, emotions

Legs—Strength, the body's support

Hands—The work of your hands, your ministry, means with which you create wealth

Feet—Your ministry, your walk in/with God, your stance with God

Loins—Reproductive part of you, can be natural children or spiritual children

References

Chapter 1

[1] Terri Seville Foy (Producer). (2016, October 26). Build Your Faith To Achieve Your Dreams [Audio Podcast]. Retrieved from http://www.itunes.apple.com

Chapter 2

[1] Academy of Poets (2017).As You Like It, Scene VII[All the world's a stage]William Shakespeare. Retrieved May 28, 2017, from https://www.poets.org/poetsorg/poem/you-dit-act-ii-scene-vii-all-worlds-stage

[2] McLeod, S. (2008).Simply Psychology: Erik Erikson. Retrieved April, 2016 from https://www.simplypsychology.org/Erik-Erikson.html

[3] Cleave(2017).Dictionary.com. Retrieved from http://www.dictionary.com/browse/cleave?s=t

[4] Persona (2017).Vocabulary.com. Retrieved from https://www.vocabulary.com/dictionary/persona

[5] GoodTherapy.org (2007).Inadequacy. Retrieved April 2015, from http://www.goodtherapy.org/learn-about-therapy/issues/inadequacy

Chapter 3

[1] McGee, R. S.The Search for Freedom from Destructive Emotions, Relationships& Behavior. (USA: The Official McGee Publishing Company, 2003), p. 51.

[2] Pietrangelo, A. (2015) Depression and Mental Health by the Numbers: Facts, Statistics, and You. Retrieved from: http://www.healthline.com/health/depression/facts-statistics-infographic#1

[3] McGee, R. S.The Search for Freedom from Destructive Emotions, Relationships& Behavior. (USA: The Official McGee Publishing Company, 2003), Pg. 51.

₄McGee, R. S. The Search for Freedom from Destructive Emotions, Relationships & Behavior. (USA: The Official McGee Publishing Company, 2003), Pg. 53-59.

₅McLeod, S. (2009).Simply Psychology: Defense Mechanisms. Retrieved July 20, 2015, from https://www.simplypsychology.org/defense-mechanisms.html

Chapter 4
₁The Meaning of Number 2 in the Bible.Retrieved May 1, 2015, from http://www.biblestudy.org/bibleref/meaning-of-numbers-in-bible/2.html.

₂Meanings of Numbers in the Bible, 2016. Retrieved from the Bible Study Site: http://www.biblestudy.org/bibleref/meaning-of-numbers-in-bible/4.html

₃Bible Study Tools (2017).Lazarus. Retrieved May 25, 2017, from http://www.biblestudytools.com/dictionary/lazarus/

Chapter 5
₁Bible Study Tools (2017).The KJV New TestamentGreek Lexicon: kategoros. Retrieved June 21, 2017, from http://www.biblestudytools.com/lexicons/greek/kjv/kategoros.html

₂Bible Study Tools (2017).The KJV New TestamentGreek Lexicon: Antidikos. Retrieved May 6, 2017, from, http://www.biblestudytools.com/lexicons/greek/kjv/antidikos.html

Chapter 6
₁All About Philosophy (2002). Materialism. Retrieved June 6, 2017, from http://www.allaboutphilosophy.org/materialism.htm

Chapter 7
₁Anderson, N. T.Victory Over The Darkness: Realizing the Power of Your Identity In Christ(Ventura, California: Regal Books From Gospel Light, 2000), p. 74.

Chapter 8

[1] NAACP (2008).Criminal Justice Fact Sheet. Retrieved July 29, 2014, from http://www.naacp.org/pages/criminal-justice-fact-sheet

[2] Proctor, B. [Proctor Gallagher Institute]. (2016, April 14). Paradigm Shift: An In-depth Explanation [Video File].Retrieved June 6, 2017, from https://www.youtube.com/watch?v=z2IEiYM_iYM

[3] Joseph P. (Producer). (February 19, 2016). Right Believing [Audio Podcast]. Retrieved from http://itunes.apple.com

Chapter 9

[1] Bible Hub (2004–2017) Yehoshua: Strong's Concordance 3091. Retrieved April 28,2017, from http://biblehub.com/hebrew/3091.htm

[2] Bible Hub (2004-2017) Iesous: Strong's Concordance 2424 Retrieved April 28, 2017, from httphttp://biblehub.com/str/greek/2424.htm

Chapter 11

[1] Sonshi Group (2017).Sun Tuz's The Art of War-Original, accurate, and complete translation of all 13 chapters. Retrieved May 2017, from https://www.sonshi.com/original-the-art-of-war-translation-not-giles.html

[2] Sonshi Group (2017).Sun Tuz's The Art of War—Original, accurate, and complete translation of all 13 chapters (chapter 1). Retrieved May, 2017, from https://www.sonshi.com/original-the-art-of-war-translation-not-giles.html

Chapter 12

[1] Reality(1828).Merriam Webster Dictionary. Retrieved from https://www.merriam-webster.com/dictionary/reality

[2] Colainno, P. (2013).The Overwhelmed Brain Personal Growth for Critical Thinkers. Retrieved May 2017 from http://theoverwhelmedbrain.com/perceptions/

[3] Seasons (1999).An Ancient Hebrew Research Center. Retrieved April 2015, from http://www.ancient-hebrew.org/56_home.html

[4] The Bible Study Tools (2017). The NAS New Testament Greek Lexicon: Phos, Strong's 5457. Retrieved April, 2015, fromhttp://www.biblestudytools.com/lexicons/greek/nas/phos.html

Chapter 13

[1] Epictetus: Making Proper Use of Impressions (1995). Internet Encyclopedia of Philosophy: A Peer Review Academic Resource. Retrieved from http://www.iep.utm.edu/epictetu/#SH4d

[2] Epictetus (2001).Brainy Quotes. Retrieved June, 2017, from https://www.brainyquote.com/quotes/quotes/e/epictetus106298.html

Chapter 14

[1] Beck, J. (2016) The Running Conversation in Your Head: What a close study of "inner speech" reveals about why humans talk to themselves. Retrieved from https://www.theatlantic.com/science/archieve/2016/11/figuring-out-how-and -why-we-talk-to-ourselves/508487/

[2] Beck, J. (2016) The Running Conversation in Your Head: What a close study of "inner speech" reveals about why humans talk to themselves. Retrieved from https://www.theatlantic.com/science/archieve/2016/11/figuring-out-how-and -why-we-talk-to-ourselves/508487/

Chapter 15

[1] Patheos (2008). Christians Crier For Ye That Have Ears?? to Hear: What Does the Number 7 Mean or Represent in the Bible.Retrieved February 21, 2017, from http://www.patheos.com/blogs/christiancrier/2014/09/26/what-does-the-number-seven-7-mean-or-represent-in-the-bible/

₂Seventy (1988).New Foundation Ministries: The Types and Symbols of the Bible. Retrieved February 2017, from http://www.newfoundationpubl.org/types.htm

Chapter 16
Stephen (2009).LDS Women of God: The Word Stone or Rock in Hebrew. Retrieved April 8, 2015, from http://www.ldswomenofgod.com/2009/11/01/the-word-stone-or-rock-in-hebrew/

Chapter 17
₁Messengers of the Name (2017).Yahuwah, This Is My Name Forever. Retrieved February 19, 2017, from http://www.messengerofthename.com/yahuwah-name-forever

₂Hebrew Streams (2017).The Hebrew Meaning of Jesus. Retrieved March 5, 2017, from http://www.hebrew-streams.org/frontstuff/jesus-yeshua.html

₃Bible Study Tools (2017).The KJV New Testament Greek Lexicons: Pneuma. Retrieved April 20, 2017, from http://www.biblestudytools.com/lexicons/greek/kjv/pneuma.html

Chapter 18
₁Bible Study Tools (2017).The NAS New Testament Greek Lexicon: SoterionStrong's Number 4991. Retrieved March 1, 2017, fromhttp://www.biblestudytools.com/lexicons/greek/nas/soteria.html

₂Bible Study Tools (2017).The NAS Old Testament Hebrew Lexicon: Yashuwah Strong's Number 3444. Retrieved March 1, 2017, http://www.biblestudytools.com/lexicons/h

₃Prosperity (2017).Google. Retrieved March 5, 2017, from https://www.google.com/webhp?sourceid=chrome-instant&rlz=1C1CHBH_enUS697US699&ion=1&espv=2&ie=UTF-8#q=define+-prosperity&*

[4]Bible Study Tools (2017).The NAS Old Testament Hebrew Lexicon: Yashuwah Strong's Number 3444. Retrieved March 1, 2017, http://www.biblestudytools.com/lexicons/h

[5]Bible Study Tools (2017).The KJV Old Testament Hebrew Lexicon: PreservationStrong'sNumber 4241. Retrieved March 1, 2017, from http://www.biblestudytools.com/lexicons/hebrew/kjv/michyah.html

[6]Preservation (2017).Dictionary.com LLC. Retrieved March 5, 2017, from http://www.dictionary.com/browse/preservation?s=t

[7]Neff, D. (2013) Biblical Adoption Is Not What You Think It Is. Retrieved May 2017, from http://www.christianitytoday.com/ct/2013/december/heirs-biblicaliblical-take-on-adoption.html?start=1

[8]Vocabulary.com (2017).Adoption. Retrieved May 2017, from http://www.vocabulary.com

Chapter 19

[1]Wikipedia The Free Encyclopedia (2017). Maslow's Hierarchy of Needs. Retrieved April 2,2017, fromhttps://en.wikipedia.org/wiki/Maslow%27s_hierarchy_of_needs

[2]Wikipedia The Free Encyclopedia (2017). Maslow's Hierarchy of Needs Image. Retrieved April 2, 2017, fromhttps://en.wikipedia.org/wiki/Maslow%27s_hierarchy_of_needs

[3]Wikipedia The Free Encyclopedia (2017). Maslow's Hierarchy of Needs. Retrieved April 2, 2017, fromhttps://en.wikipedia.org/wiki/Maslow%27s_hierarchy_of_needs

[4]Palermo, E (2014).Why Does the Moon Shine? Retrieved May 28, 2017, from http://www.livescience.com/45979-why-does-the-moon-shine.html

ORDER INFORMATION

To order additional copies of this book, please visit
www.redemption-press.com.
Also available on Amazon.com and BarnesandNoble.com
Or by calling toll free 1-844-2REDEEM.

www.ingramcontent.com/pod-product-compliance
Lightning Source LLC
Chambersburg PA
CBHW071209230425
25590CB00013B/596